PRAISE FOR
UNLEASH YOUR RISING

"The exercises and tools in this book will set your life in an upward direction and inspire you to become a more reverent leader. *Unleash Your Rising* will challenge you to be honest with yourself and activate a vision that can impact the world."

—**Jack Canfield**, Co-Author of *The Success Principles*^{TM}
and *Chicken Soup for the Soul*®

"*Unleash Your Rising* is a game-changer in personal development. No matter what you are aspiring to do, Christine Gail will unleash the part of you that feels like it isn't possible and flip the switch in your mind to make it a reality."

—**Les Brown**, World-Renowned Motivational Speaker, Best-Selling
Author of *Laws of Success* and *It's Not Over Until You Win!*

"Want a true, introspective book that will rock your world? *Unleash Your Rising* is it. Be ready for an amazing journey in story, emotional intelligence, and mindset. Whatever you are intending, you will find confidence within these pages."

—**John Assaraf**, Founder and CEO of NeuroGym^{TM}
New York Times Best-Selling Author of *Having It All*
and Best-Selling Author of *Innercise*

"This is a book that hits you on so many levels and a book that made me stop more than a few times to examine my own life and look at where I could change. I love the concept of 'Your Story' and how to look at your current story, set a new intention, and write a new story. This alone makes it worth the read. However, it goes much deeper by delving into our intentions, word choices, affirmations, and beliefs. It shows how these all affect what we receive in life, and how we can change our lives when we change our intentions. The other sections on your brain, your health, and self-leadership all go to make this book a must have on your self-improvement bookshelf and one that you will dip into again and again. Christine has written a roadmap that will start from today and last for the rest of your life."

— **Steven Aitchison**, Author of *The Belief Principle,* Founder of Your
Digital Formula and the blog *Change Your Thoughts, Change Your Life*

"I believe in a book that combines all aspects of life.... This book does exactly that and more. Christine Gail will move you with story and empower you to believe anything is possible if you are willing to overcome what has set you back in the past. I recommend *Unleash Your Rising* for people who want to change their mindset and their hearts to believe in something greater!"

— **Megan Unsworth**, Co-Founder and
First Lady of Life on Fire™, Success Coach

"Christine Gail's dive into crafting your story takes you beyond the page and into the hierarchy of personal development. Her step-by-step system to move your story of a painful past to joy and peace will not only liberate the book that is within you, but will also free you into the future you have always dreamed of creating."

— **Kimberly Spencer**, High Performance Coach
and Founder of Crown Yourself™

"Christine Gail's *Unleash Your Rising* breaks down personal growth and leadership into a unique and cutting-edge chart that allows you to unleash your true calling. It approaches leadership and personal development from all aspects of the mind, body, and soul and provides an inspirational look at how your intuition, emotion, and behavior affect your daily life. This book allows you to self-reflect, break through negative habits, and create inspired action to live the life you want."

— **Jenn Beninger**, CEO and Co-Founder of Genius Unlocked
Coaching Institute, Master Certified Coach, Trainer, and Speaker

"This book is an ebullient, heartfelt outpouring, which offers sound advice on spiritual 'self-leadership': itself a paradoxical phrase of considerable value. It is enriched by numerous quotations from masters in this field, tending to an overarching summative aspiration: "On the other side of grief lies a deeper understanding of love."

— **Dr. C. J. Fitter**, PhD, Professor of English, Rutgers University

"Christine Gail has woven her own story seamlessly into her message. It's obvious she has deeply lived what she is teaching, which is one thing that makes her book so powerful and memorable. Reading *Unleash Your Rising* is a life-changing experience that I highly recommend to anyone looking for healing and transformation in all aspects of life."

— **Lynn Weimar**, RN, MSN, Fit Beyond Fifty

"Christine Gail is creating a movement with this message. If people read and apply the core concepts of *Unleash Your Rising*, they will be surprised of the shifts they experience. I recommend this book to anyone who knows deep within there is more for their life."

— **Steven Webb**, Author of *Choosing Nothing*,
Founder of Your Inner Peace Academy

"This is a remarkable book, not only written skillfully but with a rare mix of loving attention, practical wisdom, courage, honesty, and, above all, love. I stand in awe of Christine's gentle voice as both writer and teacher."

— **Dr. Vidya Reddy**, ND, Author of *Your Journey Beyond Your Mind, Meditation Journal* and Founder of Naturally Happy

"*Unleash Your Rising* deals with one of the most powerful, yet over-looked aspects of leadership and that is the concept of self-leadership. Using her engaging writing style, Christine has given us the keys to not only understand self-leadership, but also to implement and make it part of who we are as human beings. As a coach, and as a person constantly on the lookout for ways to up my game and that of my clients, this book and the tools it offers will be one of my go-to resources for years to come. Everyone who wants to up-level their life should consider this a must read!"

— **Michael Mushlin**, Chief Increase Officer at Increase Coaching and Co-Founder of Underground Funnel Secrets

"Christine Gail's *Unleash Your Rising* is a beautifully articulated jolt of energy for the creative mind. Equally beneficial for aspiring and working artists, her simple, intuitive, and emotionally-driven method sparks entirely new ways of thinking about one's story—and oneself."

— **Aaron Mendelsohn**, Secretary-Treasurer, Writers Guild of America West and Professor of Screenwriting, Loyola Marymount University

"*Unleash Your Rising* is one of the most inspiring personal development books I have read in a very long time. Christine Gail dives deep into what is holding you back from living in your highest leadership capability. The journaling exercises and action steps lead you to your breakthrough. Immersing yourself in this book will transform your life and how you lead!"

— **Patrick Snow**, International Best-Selling Author of *Creating Your Own Destiny*

Unleash YOUR
RISING

Lead with Intention and Ignite Your Story

CHRISTINE GAIL

AVIVA
PUBLISHING
New York

Unleash Your Rising: Lead with Intention and Ignite Your Story

Aviva Publishing
Lake Placid, NY
518-523-1320
www.avivapubs.com

Christine Gail
www.ChristineGail.com
christine@unleashyourrising.com

Every attempt has been made to source all quotes properly.

For additional copies or bulk purchases visit:
www.UnleashYourRising.com

Editors: Tyler Tichelaar and Larry Alexander, Superior Book Productions
Cover Design and Interior Layout: Fusion Creative Works
Graphic Design: Sherdellah Designs
Author Photo: Brooke Preece Portrait

Cataloging-in-Publication Data is on file at the Library of Congress
Hardcover ISBN: 978-1-947937-96-3

10 9 8 7 6 5 4 3 2 1

First Edition, 2019

Printed in the United States of America

To Grace and Elizabeth.
You have my heart and support forever.

CONTENTS

INTRODUCTION

If you have picked up this book, you likely feel drawn to something within these pages. A greater purpose is here, ready to unfold for you if you are open to it. I feel an incredible connection to you as my reader, and I want to send you this message: You are made with perfect intention, and there is a grander purpose for your life. You are beautiful. You are awe-inspiring. You are a leader. Do you see it? I see your beauty, your authenticity, and all that is amazing about you. Are you congruent with these babblings of praise? What if you don't feel this way about yourself? What if instead you feel like every day you are hitting a brick wall that is blocking your growth? You may see a glimpse of your future self living your highest potential, but you can't seem to connect to it. You have a string of good days in your business, your personal life, your health, or in your relationship, but just as quickly as you build up momentum and begin to feel good, you are thrown a curveball that wipes you out. You feel like you are so far from your vision.

Do you find yourself on this roller coaster? If so, I ask that you search high up—that you go to your core knowing. Take a few deep breaths up and settle in to your intuition. Can you feel that you are grand, important, full of purpose, inner beauty, inner strength, vibrancy, good health, and happiness? If you could whisk away all the clouds that cover up that feeling, do you feel a sense of peace, love, joy, and reverence for it all? Do you feel that, if given the appropriate tools, you could easily tap into this natural state of being in all areas of your life? Do you feel you could ignite your relationships, your leadership capability, your health, your brain power, your creativity, and your ability to attract abundance? If so, then likely this book will further change your life. If not, you may not be ready for transformation. I hope you are. I am glad I was open to changing back in 2005 when I started asking the deeper questions of life, including "What is my purpose?" and "Why am I here?" If you find yourself asking these questions, then this book may be the beginning of finding the deeper answers you are searching for.

Within this book, I will not only be including my story and the stories of others, but I will also be quoting from various sources and including scientific data and insight from modern thought leaders and scientific researchers. It is through my curiosity and willingness to research how the brain works, the power of emotional intelligence, and various methods of healing that I have gained the knowledge and ability to overcome the fears and unconscious belief systems that have held me back in the past and to allow this message to flow through me in the way of a book.

This book will outline what is possible to lead a more fulfilling life, and it will give you the foundation necessary to lead others. It is meant to be a resource so you can, step by step, move into higher levels of intention in order to live your life deeply connected to the deeper meaning and purpose in your story.

"Unleashing your rising" means a variety of things, depending on where you are in your journey. If you are struggling or feeling stuck and you are continuing to see the same painful experiences show up in your life, then you will be met there. If you have moved beyond your past for the most part and are beginning to see glimpses of what is possible for a more joyful life, then this book is the appropriate fit for the stages ahead of you. If you are in the workforce or a stay-at-home parent and have been searching for something more meaningful in your life outside of your work and family, this book will ignite deeper purpose for you, help you discover the creative parts of yourself that lie dormant, and help you show up stronger and more joyful in all you do in your family and work. If you work as an executive, coach, or entrepreneur, this book will speak to how you can rise into more reverent parts of your story and become a stronger leader. If you are a creative freelancer looking for ways to enhance the altruistic parts of yourself and use your story as a means to further ignite your creativity and further transform yourself and the world, you are in the right place.

Here are some of the topics we will explore in this book.

LEADERSHIP

The foundation of this book covers two levels of leadership:

1. **Self-leadership**: This includes loving yourself, being true to your voice, discovering parts of yourself that have been lost, and healing the parts of your story that keep you from your greatness.

2. **Leading with intention**: This goes hand in hand with how you lead yourself. This includes intrinsic intention, mean-

ing how you show up in your way of being, and extrinsic intention, meaning the daily mindful steps you take, your ability to build vision, collaborate, celebrate, be resilient, and truly connect with others.

RELATIONSHIPS

In this book, you will discover how you will attract and show up in your relationships based on what story you are living in. Much of what is covered in this book is built around understanding your stories of intention and igniting your story through self-improvement and leadership. All of this transfers into the types of relationships you find yourself attracting. The relationship you have with yourself will in turn impact all the relationships you have in your work, family, friendships, and in love.

VIBRANT HEALTH

What if you were living at your greatest health potential every day? Scanning all parts of your body today, what parts are functioning well at high capacity and what parts are lacking vibrancy? How do you balance the scale in your favor for vibrant healthy aging? What steps are you taking to create balance in your life so your health does not fall victim to stress? What if you discovered your ultimate health potential? Imagine feeling full of energy, your body healing naturally and more rapidly. Would you become more accomplished? This book will offer you the secrets to a strong, healthy body and mind so you can live fully unleashed as you rise into your potential.

BRAIN EMPOWERMENT

Here is where brain empowerment comes in. If your ultimate health is unleashed, your brain will simultaneously function better. Three aspects about your brain that will be covered in this book are:

- How to improve your cognition, focus, and memory.

- Your conscious thoughts and emotions.

- Your unconscious belief systems.

This book breaks down how the brain works and how to rewire parts of your brain that are not serving you. By unleashing full brain empowerment, you will have the understanding and the tools to process emotion better, so when something hits, it doesn't take you down for days. You will feel more alert and energized throughout the day because the hardware running in the background has been cleaned up. How would it feel to no longer have mental or emotional attachment to past traumas or failures? Your belief systems will change to serving you rather than weighing you down. You have the tools to connect to your vision daily so you become more successful. Your creativity becomes ignited. You feel good! Your brain will support your mission.

INSPIRED CREATIVITY

Do you feel you are creative? So many people believe they do not have a creative bone in their bodies. I will be challenging you to think about creativity in a different way. If you consider that everything you do, everything you say, and every experience and interaction you have is a creative act, it changes everything.

Another way I will be asking you to stretch your belief about creativity is to consider that creativity and spirituality go hand in hand. When you become an instrument for creativity, you allow spirit to move through you. The more strongly connected you are in spirit, the more creative you can become. Everyone can begin to feel more deeply creative and develop a stronger spiritual connection using the tools in this book.

ABUNDANCE

This book is a call to action that will lead to an abundant life. Reading this book may shift the way you view abundance. If you follow the guided writing exercises in this book and apply all the principles, you will begin to feel freer and to embody an awareness that is tapped into the ease and flow of abundance. Overall, by using the tools in this book that help you move from disempowerment to reverence, you will become a magnet for abundance, creating a feeling of freedom, a deeper love for yourself and others, and the ability to tap into a flow of resources and synchronistic connections. Your ability to attract money will also increase as you apply the principles and exercises in this book.

My intention is to paint the picture of what your life would be like if you lived fully unleashed, rising into greater purpose and the most reverent parts of your story. You will feel whole, complete, alive with intention, and fully ignited in all areas of your life. Naturally, you will begin and end each day in gratitude. You will appreciate the challenges that each day brings as a lesson, and you will leave the disempowering emotions behind. You will find you are able to love others more deeply and more profoundly because you have a deeper and more profound love for yourself. If you are single, attracting the love of your life unfolds for you as you direct your intention toward becoming the best version of yourself. This goes for relationships as well. The ones that serve you will deepen. The ones you already know deep down don't serve you will fall away. The friendships you attract will ignite you. They will support your vision and be based in love and reverence. You will show up stronger as a leader because you will feel connected to everyone. You will serve from the space of reverence rather than from disempowerment. Since you will understand the value of integrity and intention in all aspects of your life, your new abundant mindset will positively impact your business and how you show up in leading others.

YOUR STORY OF INTENTION

This book includes a chart to help put into perspective your entire life story and to help propel you into a more joyful and abundant life. This chart is *Your Story of Intention* and it can be downloaded at www.UnleashYourRising.com/resources. There are three layers to this story:

1. Your story of disempowerment.
2. Your story of unleashing your voice and greater purpose.
3. Your story of reverence.

Placing intention within these three different levels will render three different results. Your level of joy and success depends on where you are in your own story. Your definition of joy and success may change as you climb into higher levels in your story. How you lead yourself, lead your household, and lead in your work will change as you rise into higher levels of your story. In learning about *Your*

Story of Intention, you will become aware of where you are in your own story, and you will begin to see where there is room for growth and expansion.

Invitation

This book is an invitation to honor the part of yourself that feels called to become a better leader and discover more meaning in your life. I will be inviting you to scan all areas of your life where you have been out of integrity with the still quiet voice that speaks to you when you ask a question. This is an invitation to release what is holding you back so you can stand in your creative genius. Lastly, this book is an invitation to lead your life, relationships, and work with reverent intention and build out a new vision for your life.

Rewards of This Journey

- A clearer understanding of how you can tap into the flow of abundance.

- A deepened intuition and payoff when you listen to it.

- Confidence to take steps toward honoring your creativity.

- The ability to attract deep and meaningful relationships.

- The inspiration to ignite your story.

- The courage to unleash a greater vision for your life.

- A feeling of wholeness and completeness that translates into how you lead yourself and others.

In this book, I will meet you where you are and equip you with the tools and awareness to lead a visionary life. I believe that now, more than ever, people are being called to rise into their voices and reverent states of being with intended actions to serve the world's transformation. I invite you to take this journey.

Now more than ever, people are being called to rise into their voices and reverent states of being with intended actions to serve the world's transformation.

Are you ready to unleash your rising?

CHAPTER 1

Your Story Matters

*When we deny the story, it defines us. When we own
the story, we can write a brave new ending.*

– BRENÉ BROWN

One of the first beliefs I would like you to try on in reading this book is the belief that your story matters. You came into this world to make your mark, and every experience in your life adds to the blueprint sketched out on drafting paper that eventually leads to building a magnificent castle. Each room holds a story, and oh, yes, there are skeletons in the dark dungeon, yet the beauty of the architecture, the majestic ceilings, the delicate details of the stunningly crafted gardens, down to the carefully selected drapes and antique furniture within, hold a magic ignited when the sun rises upon it. You may be reading this and thinking, *There's no way my life can be compared to the blueprint of a castle. My entire life is more like the dark dungeon.* I can guarantee that your story will be unleashed as you face that darkness and acknowledge that your story matters, has purpose, and there is an intention behind it all. This book will take you on a journey of self-discovery, and this chapter presents the beginning steps to help you ignite your story and realize that the entire blueprint of your life, including the darkness, is a force to be reckoned with.

You may say, "Well, no one would want to hear my story unless I had already made a name for myself." I believe it is an absolute myth that no one wants to hear your story unless you are famous. Your greatest gift to the world is through your story. Without story, how will people know who you are, where you came from, and why they should want to get closer to you or work with you? Many people don't even realize they have a story. Either that, or they know they have one, but they are embarrassed or ashamed of theirs. They do not see the power in their pain. Rumi, a thirteenth-century Persian poet, said, "The wound is where the light enters." When we can see the light in our pain, we can then shine as an inspiration for others.

Your greatest gift to the world is through your story.

It took me years to embrace this notion. I never told my story because I didn't want people to perceive me as a victim and I was still living in the pain of childhood abandonment, abuse, and isolation. I didn't know how to change the perception of my story and move past it, so I kept it all inside. I felt that my blueprint was the castle dungeon and that normal people lived in the castle above me. There was no way I was exposing the skeletons that lay within my soul. Only a few people in my early adult life knew I'd had a challenging childhood. I had since taken on a life that I thought looked like success, and I really, truly just wanted to feel connected to people and for people to show me whom they truly were so I could do the same.

I was walking around feeling very isolated, like I didn't fit in. I began to learn, little by little, year after year, how to break through and release the emotions related to my story, but I still felt alone. I longed for community. As I began to dive into personal development and leadership events, both as a participant and a leader, I discovered, to my surprise, that deep down everyone feels isolated in some way and everyone craves true connection with themselves and other people.

When we are able to open ourselves up in vulnerability, we find our authentic power. This is what the world is waiting for. As Brené Brown writes in *Daring Greatly*:

> When we spend our lives waiting until we're perfect or bulletproof before we walk into the arena, we ultimately sacrifice relationships and opportunities that may not be recoverable, we squander our precious time, and we turn our backs on our gifts, those unique contributions that only we can make. Perfect and bulletproof are seductive, but they don't exist in the human experience.

It can be exhausting, and it certainly doesn't serve us or anyone else to go through life playing it safe and putting on a front that we've always had all the answers. People forget what they have overcome and what they have accomplished. People forget to celebrate life because they are constantly looking for the next big thing or they are too humble to let people know what they have overcome and how incredible they truly are. Some people truly get tired of telling their stories because it gets old for them. What they may not realize is it is time to craft a new story for their lives!

CATHARTIC WRITING

The only way to begin crafting a new story is to write down your story. Every time you write your story, it becomes a cathartic process and you will build a more positive perception of it. I made a habit of writing each time I was either stuck emotionally or when I had a breakthrough. I want to encourage you to begin telling your story so it comes alive for you again. Write down all you have accomplished, each loss, each win, each fall, and each rise. Start by just writing it down. Don't worry about what it looks like—the grammar, the spelling, whether or not it is perfect or good enough. It is important that you have no agenda if this is the first time you are writing your story. Don't worry about how you would craft it into a book or into your business. Write from your heart. Just get it down on paper. If you are blocked, write through it. Just write. Just write. Just write. No matter what comes up. Just write. You will find that by just writing it all out, you will gain confidence in the process and you may find things that come up for you that require healing. You may find you are writing from a place of disempowerment. If you are writing in sadness, in anger, from a place of shame or unworthiness, just allow it. Writing it out will allow you to be unleashed from it and see the bigger picture of it all.

Tools throughout this book will help you when you get stuck or if you realize you have not healed from a part of your story. Just keep reading through the book, apply what you see that is in alignment with the breakthrough you have been searching for, and continue to write consistently.

When you feel satisfied you have written all of your story, you can work on crafting it and weaving it into your self-development book, leadership book, health and wellness book, business book, screenplay, or as the story that makes your personal, business, and client relationships more heartfelt and authentic.

HOW THE BRAIN PROCESSES STORIES

Before we dive into crafting your life story or your business story, let's first shift a little bit and talk about how our brains process stories. It is common for people to believe that stories speak to the creative side of our brains: the right side. In actuality, stories appeal to the left side of the brain, the logical side of processing information. While we craft our own personal stories in the creative side of the brain, when we tell our stories, people "hear" them from the objective left side of their brains. This is the side of the brain that puts logical things together to make a decision. So when you are telling your story, people are buying into you and breaking it down in their brains logically that they like and trust you. If they like and trust you, likely they will want to get to know you better. These are the people who will want to work with you. All in all, we humans *love* a good story. Telling your story is a way to connect with a stranger. It brings out the humanity in us. It evokes compassion in us for the person telling the story. An invisible thread of connection is woven when we evoke emotion and match common experiences. When you are hearing a story, you automatically begin to put yourself into the story, and before you know it, you have lost track of time—like zoning out while watching a movie. On top of that, scientifically-speaking, stories stimulate oxytocin production in our bodies. Oxytocin is the same hormone released in breastfeeding, love-making, and hugs. It can be a powerful persuasion tool. Basically, no matter what you are doing in your work, you must tell more stories. People want to know about you and what made you so passionate about the work you do.

When you are telling your story, people are buying into you and breaking it down in their brains logically that they like and trust you.

SETTING INTENTION FOR YOUR STORY

Before you craft your story, you must first set your intention behind it and ensure you are in a state of reverence toward your story to achieve the effect you want. Telling your story is not about you. It is about the people you will impact. This is a world transformation and it begins with your story. The end goal is to awaken and transform people in some way.

INTENTION EXERCISE:

How do you intend to impact others with your story?

_____

_____

_____

_____

_____

EPIPHANY STORYTELLING

While infusing reverent intention into your story, how do you pull out golden nuggets to build your story in a way that resonates with people? One of the simplest ways is to talk about what life used to be like for you. Then talk about your epiphany or aha moment. Next, paint a picture of how that made you who you are. Lastly, describe how your story can benefit others.

Think about the classic television commercial for Bounty paper towels. First frame shows a baby spilling a huge mess of cranberry juice onto a white floor and the mother failing miserably to clean it up with thin paper towels that turn into a soggy blob of mess. Next frame shows the aha moment: The quicker picker-upper paper towels come to the rescue, soaking up all the juice in one swipe while staying intact. Next frame is a smiling mother and a little baby crawling around on the clean floor. This story makes everyone want to use those paper towels, right?

EPIPHANY STORY EXERCISE:

You can craft your story using this simple formula:

Back then I:

_____

_____

_____

My epiphany or turning point was:

_____

_____

_____

Now I:

_____

_____

_____

This is how my journey can help you:

_____

_____

_____

This is a world transformation and it begins with your story.

FINDING YOUR VERTICAL

Another format to follow if you are building your brand with a book or a business and you do not want to be solely dependent on your personal story is to discover your vertical or something that makes you stand out. How is what you have to say different from what everyone else says? How is your message, product, or service unique? What are you doing differently that no one else in your industry knows anything about? Do you have a bold message that will wake people up from their old way of thinking or help them break away from the way things have always been done? What proof can you show—i.e., research, experience, success stories—that will inspire people?

The perfect example for finding one's vertical is seen in Albert Einstein's story. Einstein was far from the stellar student and his professors never took him seriously. After graduating from the Swiss Polytechnic Institute, Einstein spent decades researching and making bold claims while the rest of the scientific community scoffed and disagreed. He thought about dropping out of college to sell insurance! Imagine going to a networking event where Albert Einstein stands up and introduces himself, "Hello, I am Albert Einstein, and I sell life insurance." Despite these setbacks, Einstein ended up revolutionizing the way the world views light, space, gravity, and time. One of Einstein's bold claims was that "Everybody is a genius. But if you judge a fish by its ability to climb a tree, it will live its whole life believing that it is stupid."

Einstein was an innovative thinker who shook things up in the scientific and philosophical community. Like Einstein and other visionaries, you must stand out and make bold claims in your message.

FINDING YOUR VERTICAL EXERCISE:

How can you shake things up in your industry? What bold claims can you make?

_____

_____

_____

_____

_____

HOW TO CRAFT YOUR STORY

One of the most impactful books I have ever read about story is *The Seven Basic Plots* by Christopher Booker. It helps you pinpoint what type of plot your story fits into. These plots work for writing a book, screenplay, or crafting a story for your business. Here are five of the plotlines to think about when crafting your story:

1. Overcoming the Monster

This is the classic David and Goliath story where you experience something seemingly greater than you that you courageously overcome. Likely, we all have experienced at least one of these monsters: depression/anxiety, cancer, loss of a loved one, trauma, divorce, abuse, or addiction. I personally do not view them as monsters.

Rather, these experiences are rich lessons that lead us to discovering our higher selves and purposes, helping us to serve others. Donna Scott overcame childhood sexual abuse, went on to study psychology to become a licensed marriage and family therapist, and supports other survivors of abuse through her book *Tapestry of Trauma*. Steven Webb, known as the Inner Peace Guide, is a profound example of overcoming. He became paralyzed at the young age of eighteen and suffered major anxiety and depression for years until he discovered the power of mindfulness and meditation. He now inspires others through his book *Choosing Nothing* and leads an online Inner Peace Academy, teaching others how to overcome anxiety, sleep better, and manage stress. Gabby Bernstein, a multiple *New York Times* best-selling author and international speaker who has appeared on Oprah's *Super Soul Sessions*, talks about how hitting rock bottom and getting sober was the catalyst for her spiritual awakening.

We see a common theme in every story of overcoming. These perceived "monsters" lead us to loving ourselves and loving others more deeply. When we can take our stories of overcoming and use them as a catalyst for change for other people, it becomes our sweet spot.

When we can take our stories of overcoming and use them as a catalyst for change for other people, it becomes our sweet spot.

2. A Great Success Story

People love to root for the underdog and celebrate a rags-to-riches story. That is why films like *The Greatest Showman, Cinderella, Jerry McGuire, Homeless to Harvard*, and *Forrest Gump* resonate with us. If you have overcome bullying, poverty, disability, abuse, loss of your business, job, or home, bankruptcy, or you grew an empire from nothing, use these stories. Your story of beating incredible odds and finding a way to build a life of abundance will resonate with audiences. Meryl Streep was turned down for a role in *King Kong* at the young age of twenty-six because the director said she was ugly. Since then, as we know, she has had one of the most celebrated careers in Hollywood and has been nominated for a record twenty-one Academy Awards. Walt Disney was fired from the *Kansas City Star* in 1919 because his editor said he "lacked imagination and had no good ideas." It was no easy climb for Disney, as his animated shorts of Mickey Mouse failed to gain distribution. Disney, of course, did catch on and his work finally took off, turning into a multi-billion-dollar business today. Talk about vision! We all know the author J. K. Rowling. She overcame an abusive marriage and major depression, yet still managed to write the first two Harry Potter books as a struggling single mother. A few years later, her poverty turned into a net worth of $1 billion. Oprah Winfrey grew up poor as the daughter of a coal miner and a housemaid. As a child, she wore dresses made out of potato sacks, was sexually molested, and yet believed all along that she was made for something greater. After getting fired for getting emotional on air, her vision to inspire people worldwide was unleashed. She created a transformation platform through *Super Soul Sunday*, the Oprah Winfrey Network (OWN), and The Oprah Winfrey Leadership Academy for Girls (OWLAG), providing education for underprivileged youth in South Africa. I imagine if you look closely at your own life, you, too, are a success story—or one in the making.

3. The Quest

The quest is a heroic story about someone willing to sacrifice everything to search for something. We enjoy films in this genre like *The Pursuit of Happyness, Star Wars*, the Indiana Jones franchise, the Harry Potter series, and The Lord of the Rings trilogy. Gautama Buddha left his life as a wealthy prince in ancient India and renounced all material possessions and physical pleasures to focus on his quest of enlightenment. The apostles Simon Peter and Andrew in Matthew's gospel in the New Testament accepted a quest invitation from Jesus to leave Galilee and become "fishers of men." How does the quest story translate in your life? What have you been searching for? Your search for love, divine connection, peace, and your purpose are quests. The entrepreneur's journey to stand out and find solutions that meet unmet needs is a quest. I feel personally that my entire life has been a quest to discover my purpose, a deeper spiritual connection, and a more authentic connection with others. When I met Dr. Wayne Dyer in New York, his story of leaving his tenured position as a professor at St. John's University to pitch his first book, *Your Erroneous Zones*, resonated deeply. He made a bold move again when he told his publisher he was not willing to write about money and sex. Instead, he turned down an advance and wrote *You'll See It When You Believe It* about tapping into ourselves to create what we want. This began his quest to fulfill his calling to inspire people to live in their purpose. The quest story typically includes a great risk. When your audience responds with, "Wow, I don't think I could have sacrificed so much to get what I want," then you likely have a quest story.

4. Rebirth

Rebirth, prodigal son, or comeback stories may include hitting rock bottom, making a huge mistake, or an event that forces protagonists to change their ways, find themselves, or recreate themselves. Steve Jobs, known as the comeback king, was fired from his own company. He went on to collaborate at LucasFilm in the computer graphics division that later became Pixar before being rehired at Apple several years later, leading to the creation of the Mac, iPod, and iPhone. Gary Zukav, a Harvard graduate and former US Army Special Forces Green Beret, discovered his deeper spiritual purpose and wrote *The Seat of the Soul* after changing his empty life of anger, sex addiction, and experimentation with drugs. He became a *New York Times* best-selling author, and I was honored to meet him during one of his thirty-five Oprah appearances. Pastor Jurgen Matthesius, the author of *Leadersight: Seeing the Invisible to Create the Impossible* was a surfer sitting on the beach in Australia with no direction when he heard the voice of God inviting him to dive into Scripture. He listened to the voice, which continued to direct him into the ministry and an eventual move to the United States. With no savings or income, he launched numerous C3 campuses focused on replacing religion's walls with Divine relationship and community, and transforming lives through the power of the Holy Spirit. The parts of ourselves that have fallen and bounced back, or the parts of ourselves that feel no purpose, then become ignited by something bigger than us, resonate deeply within these rebirth stories: *A Christmas Carol, The Secret Garden, Rocky, How the Grinch Stole Christmas,* the story of Jesus, *What Dreams May Come*, and *Beauty and the Beast.* Where in your life have you changed and recreated yourself?

5. The Simple Story

Some people tell me, "Well, I don't have any of those kinds of stories to tell. I just live a simple life." The simplest stories of seemingly simple lives make the best stories because people resonate with the simple. Simple things speak to our hearts and our own lives. Everyone loves a simple dog story like *A Dog's Purpose* by W. Bruce Cameron or Jill Heil's children's book *Rescuing Jack and Jill*. Shows about living off the grid, simple comedies like *Friends* and *Seinfeld*, and classic children's films like *My Neighbor Totoro*, do really well because we love simple. A mentor of mine, Jenn Benninger, believed her life was so vanilla. She grew up middle class, had one brother, her parents were still married, and she was raised in a family where children were seen, not heard. After overcoming these limiting beliefs, she realized she had a voice, and part of her mission was to help others activate their own voices. Today, as a transformational coach, she helps people heal from trauma and discover that they have a voice and a mission. When you discover your voice, no matter where you came from, it naturally activates the part of you called to love and serve people.

Our stories are continuously unfolding before our eyes every moment of every day. We are living within our own stories, and as one chapter closes, another opens. Choice plays a major role in how our stories play out. I feel there is also a constant pull within and from divine intelligence guiding us to our purpose. Until we can truly listen, we continue to make the same choices, live out the same stories, and get the same results. I want to challenge you to look back on your life and discover the beauty in everything. I truly believe everyone has a powerful story that can be weaved into a book, film, or platform for a successful business. I believe you can use the background of your life and past experiences to weave a beautiful story that makes your brand more authentic and accessible. At the least, if there is just one person who is impacted by you sharing your story, you have left a legacy. Maya Angelou said it best: "Your legacy is every life you've touched."

*When you discover your voice, no matter where you
came from, it naturally activates the part of
you called to love and serve people.*

HOW TO RISE ABOVE YOUR STORY

Of course, it can be very difficult to share our stories if we have not fully healed. I experienced this earlier in my career at a speaker's workshop. I felt moved to talk about how I did not receive holiday gifts as a child. I was taught never to ask for anything from anyone, and if anyone ever gave me a birthday, Christmas, or holiday gift, my parents would insist I give it back. Imagine living your entire childhood unable to receive gifts from others. When it came time for me to consider calling upon the love and support of friends and family to support my book launch, I became very emotional. I had to ask myself, "Where is this coming from?" "What am I afraid of?"

The answer came just a few days later when my seven-year-old intuitively asked me to paint a picture of the day when I was five years old and snuck over to the neighbors' house when they weren't home to see their Christmas tree. I ended up opening up all of their Christmas presents just to experience what it felt like to open them and discover what was inside.

While I had healed the parts of myself that were resentful for being raised so differently, another layer was boiling up to the surface in need of healing: the deep-seated feeling of not enough and the inability to ask for something because all my life I had felt I didn't deserve anything. This was coming up for me because I viewed asking people for endorsements and support for my book launch as being the same as asking for and receiving a gift. There I stood in front of an intimate group of people, telling this story for the first time in public. I allowed myself to feel the fear of rejection and the not enough-ness. I felt myself freeze, and I choked up. The director of the workshop, Davide DiGiorgio, stood behind me and gently coached me: "You've got this. Go ahead. You can do this." I actually had to visualize rising up outside of my own story and becoming an observer of it to get through it and see the bigger picture. I focused on the joy I experienced at five, opening those presents, and I had an epiphany. Today, that same joy is what I feel when helping people open up the gifts of themselves. I went from feeling like I lost something to believing this experience is one reason I am writing this book.

> *I actually had to visualize rising up outside of my own story and becoming an observer of it to get through it and see the bigger picture.*

How do you get past the "in it," "stuck," "this is happening to me" part of your story, into the part where you overcome, become further unleashed, and rise above your story, wrapping it all in love, gratitude, and reverence for your journey? The first step is writing it down. Allow yourself to process it. If the story brings up emotions, allow them. When I work with clients who are experiencing these blocks, the transformation is amazing once they are able to rise above their stories and see the bigger picture using the tools in this book.

If you have a traumatic story, I encourage you to realize there is a purpose behind it. I promise you that you will find the silver lining in your story as you process it more fully and grow the courage to share it. By sharing your story, you can change lives. Your story will evoke compassion and speak to the places within us that have experienced grief. We are meant to connect with empathy on this level. This is what makes us human and helps others heal. I have personally come to realize that the grief I experienced not fitting in as a child has served as my gift for a very long time. Looking back on my past, I can see how it has made me live life bigger, love stronger, appreciate the little things, and never take anything for granted. As I help people open up the gift of who they are time and time again, I feel I am being given the greatest gift—being an instrument of change for them—and, in turn, that changes me for the better—every time.

This never-ending story is all a part of your journey toward our interconnection and the beauty of who you are meant to be in the world.

The next three chapters of this book will focus on the metamorphic experience of understanding the three different levels of story we live in called *Your Story of Intention*. As you reach the point where you can release attachment to your stories and the stories that have been thrust upon you, you can become more awake, more conscious, and more open to the greater possibilities. You will become free to imagine and create your own life. You can experience life not as attached to outcome, expectation, or what you can detect with your five senses. Your creativity and intuition will be driving the ship and you will become a more impactful leader. You can become an observer of life, surrendering to the flow and making choices based on a knowing. You will feel pulled toward certain people and experiences. You will feel connected with all people, nature, and in Spirit.

Sometimes, life will seem to be playing in slow motion around you because you have slowed down to experience life fully. You will still embrace all your stories and allow the characters within yourself, including your inner child, to express themselves. Since you become aware that these parts of yourself are not all of who you are, you can cater to them as they arise, whether they come up as triggered emotions or joyful bliss. The higher you rise in *Your Story of Intention*, the easier it will be for you to tell your stories in ways that connect people with you so they can begin to see the bigger picture of their own lives. In doing so, you are helping people discover that nothing is ever lost. This never-ending story is all a part of your journey toward our interconnection and the beauty of who you are meant to be in the world.

CHAPTER 2

Your Story of Intention,
Part 1: Disempowerment

*All the world's a stage, and all the men and women merely
players; they have their exits and their entrances,
and one man in his time plays many parts.*

— WILLIAM SHAKESPEARE, *AS YOU LIKE IT*

Another belief I would like you to try on is that you are in the spot-light on your own stage. You are in the middle of your own story, and in every moment of every day, you get to choose what role you play and how you act out your character. The world, your world, revolves around you. How you act has a ripple effect on the world around you. If you daily practice being aware of your thoughts and emotions, and put yourself in a space where you can rise above your experiences before they trigger an emotional response, your life, overall, will be more joyful and peaceful. Your intentional responses will be aligned in higher levels of unleashing and reverence. As you continue to let go of your attachment to stories that made you feel disempowered, it becomes easier to choose reverent, intentional re-sponses—it becomes your default, rather than something you are striving for. You actually embody a deeper awareness of your stories and can see the bigger picture of every experience you encounter.

You are in the spotlight on your own stage. You are in the middle of your own story, and in every moment of every day, you get to choose what role you play and how you act out your character.

Most people feel that leaving disempowering life experiences in the past is best, and rather than dealing with them when they resurface, they sweep them under the rug. The problem is, continuing to sweep them under the rug will eventually build a mountain underneath that will become impossible to avoid. This mountain of pain will become like a volcano just waiting to erupt. If you were to imagine your life as a dormant volcano, as you slice the mountain in half all the way to the core, you would see all of these unpleasant feelings and experiences like channels of lava flowing underneath. These experiences could create a volcanic eruption. This eruption could come in the form of a physical or psychological disease, a string of relationships that do not work, making choices that sabotage a relationship or career, the inability to love, trust, or connect with people, or financial instability.

As you become aware of and release what is stewing underneath, you can step into more empowering parts of your story and lead your life feeling whole and complete.

The following chart maps out *Your Story of Intention*. Consider your entire life story and the roles you play within this chart. Where have you felt disempowered? Where have you felt unleashed? Where have you risen into reverence? Every moment of every day, no matter the experience, we all have a choice to rise to higher levels of intention. As you learn the tools to unleash further, resonating within higher levels, your overall core consciousness will rise, and you will receive the gifts of reverence, including the ability to hear more clearly the still, quiet voice of your intuition and be ignited into pure creativity.

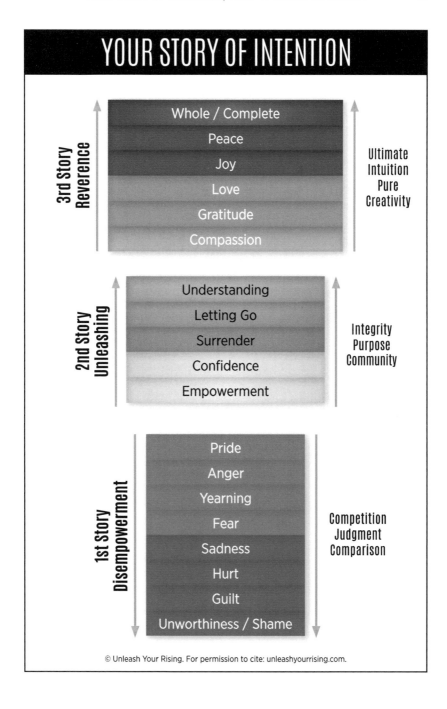

YOUR STORY OF INTENTION

3rd Story Reverence
- Whole / Complete
- Peace
- Joy
- Love
- Gratitude
- Compassion

Ultimate
Intuition
Pure
Creativity

2nd Story Unleashing
- Understanding
- Letting Go
- Surrender
- Confidence
- Empowerment

Integrity
Purpose
Community

1st Story Disempowerment
- Pride
- Anger
- Yearning
- Fear
- Sadness
- Hurt
- Guilt
- Unworthiness / Shame

Competition
Judgment
Comparison

Awareness of *Your Story of Intention* can profoundly change your relationships, your ability to lead, the way you embody your story, and your ability to attract abundance. In the rest of this chapter and in the following two chapters, I will be painting a picture of what it is like to live in these three stories and how to intend a higher state. These chapters may feel heavy, but bear with me. As the book unfolds, you will see how *Your Story of Intention* serves as the foundation for the types of relationships you attract, your ability to lead and be perceived as a leader, your perception of your story and how you tell your story, and your ability to tap into the flow of abundance. Applying the principles and exercises throughout the entirety of this book will allow you to rise into the higher states more often and unleash into your highest potential.

DISEMPOWERMENT—First Story (Competition/Judgment/Comparison):

- Anger
- Yearning
- Fear
- Sadness
- Hurt
- Guilt
- Unworthiness/Shame

FIRST STORY: DISEMPOWERMENT

The disempowerment story is where many people live and lead. Whether we are aware of it or not, we all experience phases in our lives where we process experiences from a disempowering state. It is difficult to tap into heightened creativity and intuition in this story. The levels of disempowerment range from feelings of unworthiness all the way up to action levels of competition, judgment, and comparison. Operating in the lower levels of disempowerment can be debilitating, resulting in inaction. People at these levels experience low self-esteem, self-doubt, and indifference, and they have victim thoughts and limiting beliefs. When action is taken in the higher levels of disempowerment, people are acting purely on self-fulfillment, typically experiencing exhaustion and health issues because their bodies are fueled by cortisol and adrenaline, rather than creativity and inspiration. People who operate in first story blame themselves or others for relationships, lives, or careers gone wrong. The ego is driving the ship in this story. This state is about constant striving.

FIRST STORY SIGNS

One sign you are in first story disempowerment is when your judgmental thoughts take over, whether directed toward yourself or others. You feel like you are in a vacuum, and you may experience anxiety or stress, emotional numbness, heaviness in your heart, a tightening in your throat, or migraine-like symptoms.

You may feel guilty, like everything is your fault. You may feel apathetic, hopeless, and helpless. You may feel overwhelmed with grief. You may feel boiling anger. The stage of anger is actually a good sign because to reach anger, you have to move through shame, guilt, hurt, sadness, fear, and yearning. In these lower energy states, basically, you do not feel good, and you are not consciously aware of your own story's big picture. It is impossible because it is only about you and how you are feeling in the moment. If you were to observe your thoughts, you would realize they are all self-centered. In these energy states, you are typically drowning in the emotions and making assumptions about a situation rather than focusing on the facts and reality of the story. You may have victim thoughts and wonder: "Why is this happening to me?"

As you reach the higher levels of disempowerment, you may begin to feel motivated and focused on being successful. Or you may remain stagnant and constantly in a state of comparing and judging others' successes. Either way, what typically occurs is people become stuck in this state and continue to feel divided from people because they are in competition with others. There is a sense of "us against them." In this disempowering state, your viewpoint of money and provisions is that there is not enough. You judge others for what they have and the choices they make. In a competing state, in your mind you feel above other people. You feel your life is better, your choices are better, and your belief systems are better. On the other hand, you could experience this state as a comparison feeling and take on the belief that everyone else's life is better. You may compare what they have to what you have. This keeps you stuck because you revert back to yearning, feeling unworthy, and feeling not enough. In work and business, competitive energy exists even among co-workers. In religion and spirituality, you may believe your way is the only correct way. You make judgments, both big and small, in your thoughts and verbally daily, throughout the day. You are addicted to judging others and circumstances. Gossip and complaining comes easily to you. You tend to tell the same sad stories about your life over and over like a broken record. It is difficult for you to find a common ground with people who are different from you. You surround yourself with people who are also stuck in this state. People living in disempowerment stages are looking outside of themselves for validation. The voice of intuition is buried amongst all the noise of the mind and the highly charged emotions that run rampant.

People living in disempowerment stages are looking outside of themselves for validation. The voice of intuition is buried amongst all the noise of the mind and the highly charged emotions that run rampant.

MOVING PAST COMPETITION, JUDGMENT, AND COMPARISON

Moving past the competing, judging, comparing stage is the most difficult because it is the last stage of disempowerment. We, as a society, have been conditioned to compete with one another. The fight or flight part of our brains is still steering most of our default responses. However, this system of competition and survival of the fittest is not serving the world's higher good. When disaster hits, like with the events of 9/11, Sandy Hook, a catastrophic natural disaster, or health disaster, and we come together for the restoration of a community, we get a taste of what is possible. We will continuously be called to unite together, to accept and celebrate others, no matter their stature, race, sexual orientation, or religious or political views. As we begin to see that we are all divinely intended and connected in love, the competing, judging, and comparing will fade away. We will begin to have compassion for all people, even those in disempowerment states, because we can see they are doing the best they can given their circumstances. When we witness people fall, we will be called to help them rise. When we fall, we will see it as an opportunity to learn rather than a failure. When we see people begin to rise up into a more empowered life, rather than judging them, we will celebrate what it took for them to get where they are. I invite you to make a habit of turning the competing, judging, and comparison into compassion and celebration—including becoming more compassionate and celebratory toward yourself!

When disaster hits and we come together for the restoration of a community, we get a taste of what is possible.

Living in the disempowerment stage of first story has a profound effect on your success in relationships, your leadership style, your story style, and your ability to attract abundance. The following describes what it is like to live in first story. If you are aware of yourself in these states, be gentle to yourself and follow the tools in this book to rise above them.

RELATIONSHIP STYLE: First Story Disempowerment

People stuck in disempowerment stages often attract mates that they know deep down are not good for them. If they could intuitively listen to the answers to questions like, "Is this person the right fit for me?" they would avoid years of hurt and pain. People who find themselves in toxic relationships have difficulty getting out until they step into the empowering, unleashed stages of their stories. They do not have enough love for themselves to leave, so they stay in relationships that do not serve them, and their mate becomes a match to the kind of love they feel they deserve. Most people in these relationships experience some kind of shame and self-loathing. If they do not love themselves, it is difficult to attract someone who will love and care for them. People will attract whom they believe they deserve. If they have not healed childhood trauma or grief (either from an ended relationship, lack of connection with a parent, work or financial loss, or from a loved one passing), the person will attract a mate who will bring this trauma out in them, giving them the opportunity to heal. People operating in first story are often hurt from the past, can be jealous, easily triggered, and will often compete with their partner to be seen, heard, loved, and respected. People in their disempowerment state in relationships are offended easily and are often unable to fully give or receive love. Some are wrapped up in people-pleasing based on a yearning for love and reciprocation. Disempowering relationships are not built on integrity. The physical intimacy may or may not be fulfilling; however, since there is no spiritual bond in place, the relationship typically will not have long-term stamina as the love is purely conditional.

LEADERSHIP STYLE: First Story Disempowerment

Leaders who operate in first story make it all about themselves. They typically do not connect well with their teams and feel disinterested in connecting with other leaders. Rather than focusing on how to build up the morale of their teams and improve their organization, a lot of energy is expended protecting themselves and their organization against competition and theft. Their viewpoint around money and business is that there is not enough to go around. Their leadership style can be authoritarian and based on a reward/punishment system. Their intention is to compete with others, including members of their team. All action they take is focused on power, control, gaining respect, and recognition. Their belief system is black and white without much flexibility or creative thinking. First story leaders easily judge and compare themselves to others and to the competition. They rarely give praise and are very critical. In fact, they may downplay what their team accomplishes because they fear someone may be seen as better than them or be more liked. Disempowering leaders have no loyalty for their team and feel everyone is dispensable. Leaders who operate in a disempowering state are unaware that they are the problem. Their thoughts are centered around themselves and not failing. They are in the business of building revenue, not people. They use fear-based language to attempt to motivate their teams, rather than using empowering language to build up morale.

STORY STYLE: First Story Disempowerment

When people tell or write their stories from first story, victim language prevails. Their emotions are still at the surface and can be felt in the body. Typical language in first story is, "This happened to me." In lower levels of disempowerment, they may feel abandoned by God and completely alone. It is difficult to tell their story in this state because of debilitating shame, guilt, sadness, and anger. People telling their stories in first story are still "in" their stories. Some begin to build an identity based on what has happened in their lives. "Well, this is just the hand I was dealt." "I am always unlucky in relationships." "I don't deserve to be successful." "I don't know how to be happy." "I am meant to be alone." "I don't need anyone." "This person ruined my life." "No one would want to hear my sad story." "I don't have anything worth sharing." "I just need enough to get by." "Nothing ever works out for me."

As people move into higher levels of first story, they begin to move beyond the past and allow themselves to feel and release the emotions that do not serve them. It is natural for them to begin to feel anger and to find their voices. In the top stages of disempowerment, people may begin to feel empowered by taking action, yet it is done in the energy of competition and comparison. They can become stuck in the *doing* of their lives—making money, furthering education, celebrating accomplishments, obtaining possessions, yet it is all focused on their own gain and to show others that they have risen above their circumstances. They are in constant competition with themselves and others. In this higher state of first story, it is still very easy to become bogged down in anger and other lower states within first story. People find themselves on a teeter-totter and likely do not find real fulfillment in their work and relationships.

Grief is a core aspect of how people tell and relate to their story in disempowerment. Grief is simply wanting something other than what is and longing for a void to be filled. When you compare yourself to others who have what you want, you are grieving the scarcity in your life, which typically includes past failures. When you can reframe those failures as strengths, and with gratitude, forgive yourself and others, you will be in stronger alignment with your true essence and with passion for your life. Then you will be able to experience and appreciate the present moment, where you are right now, which provides natural momentum toward seeing your story's bigger picture.

ABUNDANCE: First Story Disempowerment

Abundance comes in many forms—love, money, freedom, to name just a few—and they are all interconnected. Since I already covered relationships above, and as we all know, freedom is one of the side effects of having more money, I will focus on the money component of abundance. What typically happens in the disempowerment stages is that what you manifest often comes to you, but it will not stay. Most of the time, if you are in these lower-calibrated states, you are attempting to create something from the space of unworthiness and lack. When it comes to attracting money, in the disempowerment stage, you will have a conflicting relationship with money and find yourself constantly yearning for more in a spiral of debt and lack. In this state, your beliefs around money play the broken record of, "Money doesn't grow on trees," "Money is the root of all evil," "Money changes people," "People with money are fake and cannot be trusted," "I can't afford it," "That is too expensive," "I don't really need money," "There isn't enough to go around," and the list goes on. In first story, self-worth and unconscious beliefs about money play a significant role in your ability to attract what you want. When you begin to serve and experience life outside of your own perception, you can tap into the flow of abundance. You will realize that the more profound the impression you make in the world, the more abundant you become because you are unleashing the part of yourself that feels deserving of abundance.

The more profound the impression you make in the world, the more abundant you become because you are unleashing the part of yourself that feels deserving of abundance.

Every experience is calling you into the higher, third story of intention, the story of reverence. At any point, anyone can unleash themselves and move into higher levels, yet through choices and unconscious disempowering programming, they dip back into first story. There may be experiences where you feel a glimpse of third story, yet until you heal all your past disempowering experiences, and wrap them in love, gratitude, and reverence, it becomes impossible to hold these states. As you continue to clear out the disempowering emotions that hold you back and replace them with positive affirmations and positive actions, you open yourself up to receiving more joy. The cleaner your vessel becomes, the easier it is for you to maintain reverent states.

Every experience is calling you into the higher, third story of intention, the story of reverence.

INVITATION:

I invite you to download the color chart: *Your Story of Intention* from UnleashYourRising.com/resources and post it in your home, on your refrigerator, by your vision board, and in your work area. Any time you are experiencing disempowering states, ask yourself: What is required for me to unleash into a higher level of intention?

STEPS TO RISE UP:

Follow these steps to rise up:

> **Acknowledge (A):** Acknowledging disempowering states creates awareness.

> **Release (R):** Release of emotion creates a space for growth.

> **Intend (I):** Intention toward a higher level of awareness is the unleashing.

Scan each disempowering experience. Acknowledge how you feel. Allow yourself to feel the emotions that come up with each experience, releasing and letting go of the emotions. Depending on what the emotion is, it may help to cry it out, scream at the wall, punch a pillow, go for a walk, pray, meditate, or journal. As you process these feelings, you will likely experience other emotions within first story. Allow them all. Be gentle on yourself, realizing these feelings do not define you. You can let them go. You have been carrying around these disempowering feelings like luggage. As you release them, you can travel lighter and feel free. Now set the intention to rise above the story of these experiences and attain a higher state of awareness. Visualize wrapping the experiences in light, love, and gratitude. Honor both your part and the other person's. Now cut

the emotional cord to the experience and continue to layer in affirmations like, "I am worthy. I am loved. I have everything I need.
I am _____." Do this continuously every day until the emotions
subside and you feel released and free of the experiences. Awareness
of *Your Story of Intention* and incorporating these three steps—
Acknowledge, Release, Intend (ARI)—can profoundly change your
relationships, your ability to lead, the way you embody your story,
and your ability to attract abundance.

CHAPTER 3

Your Story of Intention, Part 2: Unleashing

The only person you are destined to become is the person you decide to be.

— RALPH WALDO EMERSON

UNLEASHING—Second Story (Integrity/Purpose/Community):

- Understanding
- Letting Go
- Surrender
- Confidence
- Empowerment

SECOND STORY: UNLEASHING

The unleashing feels invigorating and freeing, yet it does come with some work. In the unleashing, you take back power over your own life. You no longer allow anything from the past, present, or future to disempower you. You begin to realize that the thoughts in your head and the emotions you feel are not you, and with practice, you can exhibit control over your thoughts and emotions, rather than having your thoughts and emotions control you. To become fully unleashed, you must first accept 100 percent responsibility for your life so far. This does not mean you accept the blame for childhood abuse or things completely out of your control. What it does mean is you can take responsibility for allowing the past to govern your life. You have the ability to empower yourself and move past your past. Oprah once stated:

> I truly understand that there is a lesson in everything that happens to us. So I try not to spend my time asking, "Why did this happen to me?" but rather, I try to figure out why I had chosen it. That's the answer you need. It's always a question of accepting responsibility for your choices. Anytime you look outside of yourself for answers, you're looking in the wrong place.

You can take responsibility for allowing the past to govern your life. You have the ability to empower yourself and move past your past.

INTEGRITY INVENTORY

Integrity is an essential component of the unleashing. The unleashing stage is activated through integrity: integrity with your word, integrity in what you stand for, integrity with your body and health, integrity in what you feel called to do, integrity in honoring your intuition, integrity in your dealings with others, and integrity in all of your decisions.

Integrity includes taking full responsibility for past decisions that, deep down, you knew were not aligned with your highest good. As you live in integrity, you will become very intentional about how you care for your body, who you spend your time with, and how you spend your time. You develop strength in recognizing your intuition and can begin to deepen your intuition by listening when it directs you in both small and large decisions.

Once you become strong enough to live in integrity, you will begin to feel more empowered. At this stage, people find their authentic voices. You will begin to feel like a new person. You will feel as if you found yourself. You will begin to feel more motivated, and you will begin to feel more creative. In this state, it doesn't matter what everyone else is doing. You are no longer yearning for validation. You find validation within yourself, just as the person you are. This is a stage where people may hear a stronger calling to switch careers or they begin to find more joy in their current work because it is easier to connect with people.

You begin to honor what it takes to climb into higher levels as you develop more confidence in what you believe in and what you feel called to do. You may find, while you are feeling more purposeful in all you are doing at work, that you are no longer striving. Instead, there is a surrender and a knowing that everything will unfold as it is meant to. Letting go may include asking for forgiveness for past choices you made in disempowering states and forgiving others who were also operating from first story. You develop a deeper understanding for the bigger picture of your life and the world. This stage is a natural progression into developing a stronger spiritual connection.

RISING INTO UNDERSTANDING

In the higher stages of second story, you develop an understanding of the bigger picture of your life. The understanding stage of unleashing includes moving from "This happened to me" to "This happened for me." This is absolutely the greatest shift you can make. When I became aware that I was still living in my story, feeling disempowered by the way I was raised—isolated from a normal life, unable to participate in sports, dance, or theater; prohibited from having friends or attending pep rallies, football games, school dances; not allowed to try out for cheerleading; feeling the holiday celebrations torn from me; and looking longingly at other families as they created family traditions and seemed to live such happy lives while I felt so alone and so different—I realized I had to tell myself, "Stop. It is time to let these emotions go and change your perception of your story." I first felt empowered when, at sixteen, I moved in with my sister and, for the first time, learned what it was like to have a group of friends, celebrate my birthday and other special occasions, join the dance team, play basketball, run track, and get involved in the performing arts. At last, I grew into my confidence and could just be in my creative spirit and be free.

Although I saw a glimpse of empowerment at sixteen, as an adult, I still felt attached to the emotions of my past. It wasn't until many years later that I began to put all my focus on what it would take to see the power of my story and rise above it. I began to change my perception of the stories I played over and over in my mind, surrendered to the process, let go of the bitterness, and moved into a deep understanding of where my parents were coming from. Their choices to protect me from what they considered worldly influences had been made out of love. My stepmother had inherited six children by marrying my father, and then they adopted two more. She taught me how to read and write before the age of five. She taught me resilience, and she taught me self-reliance. My father, a retired master sergeant, served in the Army faithfully for twenty-five years, including two one-year tours of duty in Vietnam. He struggled to keep his family together despite chains of abuse, all the challenges within his first marriage, and the division that occurred due to his second marriage. My father showed up with the best intentions he could, given his life experiences and the example of love he had. Providing fifty acres for his children to grow up on, he gave me the freedom I needed to explore nature, ride horses, and learn responsibility. He taught me hard work, trustworthiness, and forgiveness. My biological mother also made the best choices she could, given where she was in her life and generationally. I began to understand deeply that we all go through the same emotions—only the stories are different. For me, the recurring theme was grief. I grieved the loss of my childhood, and it took changing my perception of my childhood to move past it.

TURNING GRIEF INTO PURPOSE

I first became aware of the power of grief in high school. I had experienced the emotion at a very young age when my parents split up and my mother left, but I was not aware of it, and I certainly did not allow myself to feel it. It wasn't until I was in high school and cast as the lead in the school play that I allowed myself to experience the depth of the emotion and realized its power. My senior year, after moving in with my sister, I was cast in the play, *Of Winners, Losers, and Games,* about a contest between good and evil characters representing positive and negative emotions and featuring a married couple who had lost their child. I landed the role of the mother. To prepare for the role, I looked back on all the grief I had experienced to that point and brought that into my character. On opening night, all my friends in the play spent their time backstage having fun, laughing, and goofing around. Instead, I put headphones on, listened to dramatic, classical music, and recalled every instance of grief in my past: the grief of losing a parent, the grief of not fitting in, the loss of joy when our family celebrations were taken away, the grief of not being allowed to have friends. For the first time, I allowed myself to feel the grief. I brought all this grief into my character—the woman who had tragically lost her child.

While on stage, I looked out at the audience and cried out in grief. I fully stood in the emotion with every line I spoke. The audience's reaction served as my *unleash your rising* moment. Through this character, I connected with the people in the audience. I felt their shift in emotion and their compassion toward my character's suffering. I felt their hearts open up. In *that* moment, the notion came to me loud and clear that on the other side of grief lies a deeper understanding of love. Through grief, if you allow it, you can more deeply understand what truly matters and realize your purpose.

On the other side of grief lies a deeper understanding of love.

After the play, people came up to me with their hearts open, congratulating me, some with tears in their eyes. I felt, "Aha, this is what it feels like to have an open heart and be received with an open heart. I want more of this!" I ended up winning three best actress awards for that play, until we were beat out in regionals; however, it wasn't winning the awards that unleashed my rising. Instead, it was looking out at the audience each time I stood on stage and feeling that shift in their hearts into a higher state of appreciation for their lives. A shift to love.

I had no idea back then that I had a gift for opening people's hearts or that part of my life purpose was to help others let go of grief and become unleashed into their purposes. Writing this book, I began to look back on my other experiences with grief and how they broke me down, then built me back up stronger, with more passion. As you take inventory of your grief, let it go, and move into a deeper understanding of your story; then you will be able to experience and appreciate the present moment, where you are right now. This appreciation will provide a natural momentum for elevating yourself in *Your Story of Intention* so you can see the richer purpose in your life.

COMMUNITY

This is where community comes in. This piece is very simple. As you become more aligned in your purpose, you begin to feel a deeper connection with people because simultaneously you realize that part of your purpose is to serve. You no longer feel the need to have others validate you, so you can show up with no attachments and become a magnet for their transformation as well, just by being you. Unleashing creates the ripple effect. When you unleash the joyful, purposeful essence of who you truly are, you are giving others permission to harness their own authentic strength and creative power.

Within the unleashing lies a shared responsibility and collaboration for the higher good of humanity. This is why when you embrace the process to become unleashed, the experiences and the people show up to fulfill that collaborative effort. In authentic community with other thought leaders, you can be vulnerable and offer support to one another. Community will hold you accountable in integrity with your purpose. Community builds a stronger instrument for change and is a natural progression in the stage of unleashing.

When you unleash the joyful, purposeful essence of who you truly are, you are giving others permission to harness their own authentic strength and creative power. Within the unleashing lies a shared responsibility and collaboration for the higher good of humanity. This is why when you embrace the process to become unleashed, the experiences and the people show up to fulfill that collaborative effort.

CONSCIOUSNESS AS RELATED TO YOUR UNLEASHING

Consciousness is a combination of three things:

1. Being aware of yourself, your thoughts, your emotions, and the impact you deserve to make upon the world.

2. Being in alignment with your true essence of compassion, gratitude, love, joy, and peace.

3. Aligning with your connection to God, universal consciousness, ultimate intuition, and pure creativity.

Consciousness is being more aware of your thoughts and emotions and choosing to be present in the now rather than carrying the weight of the past or being anxious or worried about the future. Interacting with people consciously is simply staying present with them in a being state, all senses engaged with what they are saying.

Consciousness is a product of the brain; however, neuroscientists cannot pinpoint where in the brain it occurs. It is a collaborative effort of the brain. Dr. David Hawkins, the author of *Power vs. Force*, had one of the largest psychology practices in New York City and became an authority in the field of consciousness research using muscle testing (applied kinesiology) to calibrate truth and the consciousness of people, places, and things. He found that most people do not grow much in their overall consciousness and remain in disempowerment states most of their lives. By using the tools in *Unleash Your Rising* and aligning yourself in a strong spiritual connection as outlined in number three above, I believe people who are truly committed to the work can move out of their disempowerment stories and begin to unleash their consciousness exponentially.

One of the first steps to moving out of disempowerment into a higher conscious state is to become aware of your breathing. Notice how your breath feels entering and leaving your body through your nose. Take three deep breaths in and out. One. Two. Three. How does that feel? Can you hold breathing awareness throughout your day no matter what you are doing or what is happening? Eckhart Tolle, author of the *Power of Now* and *A New Earth*, encourages, "Be aware of your breathing as often as you are able, whenever you remember. Do that for one year, and it will be powerfully transformative. And it's free." He makes the profound statement: "One conscious breath in and out is a meditation." Just by connecting with breath, you are connecting with the present moment and with spirit in divine connection. Even the Bible mentions that "every living thing" has "the breath of the spirit of life" (Genesis 7:21-22). Life begins with conscious breathing and connection with spirit. Life doesn't happen in our busy, thought-filled minds or in the disempowering stories we continue to tell ourselves over and over.

Life occurs right here, right now, in the present moment.

Practicing present-moment awareness can create a profound shift from disempowerment into your unleashing.

Life begins with conscious breathing and connection with spirit. Life doesn't happen in our busy, thought-filled minds or in the disempowering stories we continue to tell ourselves over and over. Life occurs right here, right now, in the present moment.

YOUR THOUGHTS AS RELATED TO UNLEASHING

What about your thoughts? In 2005, the National Science Foundation published an article regarding research about human thoughts per day. The average person has about 60,000 thoughts per day. Of those, 80 percent are negative and 95 percent are exactly the same repetitive thoughts as the day before. When your thoughts are taking over, you are living in the unconscious mind, in a disempowered state. Your disempowering emotional state fuels your thoughts; then you find yourself unconsciously reacting. Imagine if you could observe every thought in your brain and respond rather than react unconsciously?

Sigmund Freud, the founder of psychoanalysis and one of the twentieth century's most influential thinkers, illustrated the concept of the unconscious mind with an iceberg. He describes our conscious mind as the tip of the iceberg and our unconscious mind as the rest of the iceberg beneath the surface. The unconscious mind is the reactive mind, or the fight-or-flight part of the brain. This reactive mind lives in the first story disempowerment stage where emotions like shame, guilt, sadness, anger, and yearning reside. Our thoughts can either trigger the fight-or-flight response related to disempowering emotions, or they can stimulate the prefrontal cortex, where emotional regulation occurs, helping us shift into more positive states that embody empathy, love, and compassion. The amazing thing is, with practice, you can begin to observe your thoughts, change your thoughts, regulate your emotions, and rise into higher levels in *Your Story of Intention*!

———————

Rising into the unleashing stage of second story has a profound effect on the success of your relationships, leadership style, story style, and ability to attract abundance. The following describes what it is like to live in second story in these categories of your life.

RELATIONSHIP STYLE: Second Story Unleashing

As you move into second story, your relationships may change. The yearning for love outside of yourself experienced in first story begins to fade away. If you are in a relationship that does not serve you, you will begin to tap into your voice and take a stand for what is important to you. As you harness what it means to be fully in integrity with yourself, you will no longer accept disrespectful behavior, and you will begin to carve out new boundaries. It becomes important to you that your partner grows with you; otherwise, an imbalance is in place. As one partner becomes authentically empowered, it is imperative that the other partner rises up as a support and/or an equal partner in transformation. Since you no longer fear being alone, in the lower levels of the unleashing, if expectations are not met, this could mean the end of the relationship. As you reach higher levels in second story, including surrendering and letting, your expectations are replaced with appreciation for your partner's gifts and contributions. In this case, even challenging relationships can be saved because as one partner cuts the cord to attachment to how the other partner validates them, and rather focuses on their own unleashing, the other partner typically begins to take notice and rises up as well.

Relationship currency comes in different forms; for example, while one partner works, the other is doing their part in keeping the home, finances, and children in order. The most monumental epiphany in a relationship's higher levels of unleashing is allowing your partner to be who they are. Instances will come up that in the past were swept under the rug or dealt with using disempowering tactics. Until you and your partner learn the lessons you are meant to learn to bring you to unconditional love, the same issues will come up either in your current relationship or subsequent ones. As they come up, you can choose to communicate with one another, forgive, and create a new relationship built on integrity and an understanding of where each of you are coming from and where you are going together.

If you are single, overall, you no longer require validation outside of yourself. You are focused on your own personal growth and becoming more deeply connected with yourself and developing spiritually. You are not attached to meeting anyone at all. You are surrendering to the process and know that what is meant to be will unfold for you. The most important part of unleashing when single is no longer yearning and striving for a relationship. You truly become perfectly happy in your own skin.

LEADERSHIP STYLE: Second Story, Unleashing

Unleashed leaders have a strong sense of integrity toward their work and mission. They move from a "What's in it for me?" mentality, to "How can I serve?" Leaders who operate in second story are in business to build up and empower people. They are not as concerned with competing; rather, their focus is on how to provide the best service and/or product and build the most cohesive teams. These leaders have not only empowered themselves and become confident in their capabilities, but they delight in empowering others in their gifts and talents, and they enjoy seeing team members build confidence in their own leadership skills. Unleashed leaders have vision and can enroll their teams and clients in their vision. They skillfully plan out goals and budgets, yet they are able to surrender to the process. They lead intuitively and do not become emotionally tied to outcomes. Rather than managing people, they help people become unleashed in their gifts and talents. When challenges arise, they see them as opportunities to learn, improve, and collaborate with team members. Unleashed leaders understand what motivates people. Leaders operating in second story are creative and innovative.

Unleashed leaders have a strong sense of integrity toward their work and mission. They move from a "What's in it for me?" mentality, to "How can I serve?" Leaders who operate in second story are in business to build up and empower people.

STORY STYLE: Second Story, Unleashing

As you move into second story, the way you tell your story changes. To move into the unleashing, it is helpful to write your stories down and allow any disempowering emotions to come out. You may feel the need to confront people from your past or present to have authentic conversations about how their actions affected you. It may be necessary to ask for forgiveness and acknowledge others for the important roles they play in your life. These actions help you move into integrity, the first stage of the unleashing. To reach integrity, it is pertinent to scan all areas of your life and ask yourself, "Have I been true to myself and my voice?" "Have I made choices for my higher good?" "Where am I out of integrity?" As you become true to yourself and willing to revisit and heal the past, you will begin to move into authentic empowerment and build confidence to better your life.

The difference is that the actions taken in the unleashing are without the ego impulses present in first story. There is no longer a yearning at work. Instead, the yearning has been replaced with a surrendering. Layers of forgiveness begin to reveal themselves, and continued forgiveness is made possible. Telling your story from the state of unleashing, you are no longer "in" your story. Instead, you have created new neuropathways to your story by shifting your thoughts, emotions, and overall consciousness. You take the rich lessons in the story and leave everything else no longer serving you. Stories told in second story are those of overcoming and unleashing into your voice and purpose. When the past creeps up, you can continue to make the choice to forgive yourself and others. It becomes easier to let go and embody a deeper understanding of your story and where others are coming from. You are now telling your story from the present, rather than from the past. As a bonus, your creativity and intuition become stronger in the unleashing stage.

Telling your story from the state of unleashing, you are no longer "in" your story. Instead you have created new neuropathways to your story by shifting your thoughts, emotions, and overall consciousness. You are now telling your story from the present, rather than from the past.

ABUNDANCE: Second Story, Unleashing

Becoming unleashed in abundance requires you to change the way you view money. You shift from feeling there isn't enough to the belief that there is plenty to go around. You change your language around money. You understand that abundance has no beginning and no end. There is a flow to it, and you find that it flows more easily through you. Integrity is a key element to attracting abundance. Where have you been out of integrity with money? How can you develop a stronger respect for money? Integrity, in regard to what you feel called to do, is unleashed in this stage as well. You move from wanting to do just enough to get by, to seeing the bigger picture of the greater impression you intend to make. If you are willing to live a bigger story and shift from serving yourself to serving others, you will find that you can tap into the flow of abundance more easily.

If you are willing to live a bigger story and shift from serving yourself to serving others, you will find that you can tap into the flow of abundance more easily.

UNLEASHING EXERCISE:

What did this chapter stimulate for you in embodying a higher level of intention in your life? What steps are you inspired to take to unleash your relationships, your leadership style, your story style, and abundance?

_____

_____

_____

_____

_____

_____

INVITATION:

I invite you to download the color chart: *Your Story of Intention* from UnleashYourRising.com/resources and post it in your home, on your refrigerator, by your vision board, and in your work area. Any time you are experiencing disempowering states, ask yourself: What is required of me to unleash into a higher level of intention? Follow the 1. Acknowledge, 2. Release, 3. Intend Steps (ARI) mentioned in the previous chapter to rise to a new level.

Awareness of *Your Story of Intention* and incorporating the ARI steps can profoundly change your relationships, your ability to lead, the way you embody your story, and your ability to attract abundance.

CHAPTER 4

*Your Story of Intention,
Part 3: Reverence*

*Gratitude bestows reverence, allowing us to encounter everyday
epiphanies, those transcendent moments of awe that change
forever how we experience life and the world.*

— JOHN MILTON

REVERENCE—Third Story
(Ultimate Intuition/Pure Creativity):
- Whole/Complete
- Peace
- Joy
- Love
- Gratitude
- Compassion

THIRD STORY: REVERENCE

Reverence, according to the *Merriam-Webster Dictionary*, means
"honor or respect felt or shown." Reverence is a *being* state. You
don't have to do anything, but you can. When you do take action in
this state, it flows, feels effortless, and everything you need to bring
it forth shows up. You fully surrender in this space and become an

instrument for whatever message, creative art, or intuitive leadership is meant to flow through you. Your intuition is at its peak in this state. Reverence is where your highest creativity is activated. You realize everything you have ever needed to feel joyful and fulfilled is within. When you live with reverent intention, you begin to feel compassion for others, and you develop a heart to serve and make a helpful contribution. You may experience periods of peace and blissful joy, and sometimes it may feel like your heart could burst as you see people through the eyes of unconditional love.

Almost every day begins with gratitude, and if you find yourself experiencing disempowering emotions, you can quickly recognize where they originate, allow them, release them, and shift back into gratitude. As you embody reverence, an honoring of yourself and others, you become more resilient, open, and ready for change, and more forgiving, peaceful, happy, joyful, and detached from other people's behavior, society's expectations, and how others view you. In a reverent state, you can become like a peaceful newborn again. You take everything in, living in the moment. You have no judgment of anyone. You are not as attached to beliefs. Your eyes are wide, full of wonder, soaking everything in, seeing it for the first time. You have no agenda. You see the best in people. You are connected to joy.

In a reverent state, you can become like a peaceful newborn again. You take everything in, living in the moment. You have no judgment of anyone. You are not as attached to beliefs. Your eyes are wide, full of wonder, soaking everything in, seeing it for the first time. You have no agenda. You see the best in people. You are connected to joy.

Imagine if you could lead your life and lead others in this way. That doesn't mean you become widely open to anyone or anything that comes your way. Leading reverently also greatly improves your intuition and radar for what best serves you. You become more tuned in to that inner knowing about situations, people, opportunities, and how you spend your time and with whom. You are living in the present moment with a compass that directs you into greater purpose. In the moment, there is no past and no future—there is only now.

COMPASSION AND GRATITUDE

Compassion and gratitude are the cornerstones of living in joy. Moving from the understanding stage of second story to compassion is moving from the head to the heart. The most important journey you can make is the eighteen-inch journey from your head to your heart. When you can move from an understanding of where people are coming from to a feeling of true compassion, it creates an energy shift that goes beyond the intellect. When you begin to meet people with your heart rather than with knowledge, you will create a connection fused in the heart. If you are just in it for yourself and to prove yourself, anything you are intending will eventually lose momentum. Loving and serving others, you will be fueled by the beautiful intrinsic rewards that come with your karmic deposits. Compassion activates altruism—the act of giving of yourself without the expectation of something in return. This stage is where the ego is no longer driving the ship. The motivation to serve truly comes from an intrinsic desire to elevate others without a personal agenda. You become an instrument to build others up. This will become the fuel for your *aliveness*.

Compassion activates altruism—the act of giving of yourself without the expectation of something in return. You become an instrument to build others up. This will become the fuel for your aliveness.

Compassion is also a more elevated stage of letting go, of forgiveness. When you have compassion for others, even if they have caused you pain, you are embodying reverence for their journey. Compassion is a mandatory pit stop to gratitude. You can then rise into gratitude for the experience and truly honor the rich lessons weaved into that part of your journey. Gratitude is a more elevated stage of surrender. In gratitude, you have surrendered all expectation and feel truly satisfied with what you have. Gratitude creates the space for more abundance, whether that shows up in the form of love, money, meaningful friendships, or opportunities. When you live with compassion and in gratitude, you are in a reverent state, prepared to receive.

Showing up reverently requires first connecting to yourself and your story and being willing to remove or change anything that stands between you and what you feel called to do. When you infuse reverent intention with your reverent state of being, you naturally begin to follow the prompts that come through your intuition. It is a balance between living in the moment (reverent, being) and executing plans for the future (intention, doing). You have fully moved from striving to arriving. Carl Jung calls this "the afternoon of life." As you experience reverent intention, you are fully in the rhythm and flow of what is meant for you. You attract what you want easily, yet you have no attachment to what you attract. You are tapped into a flow of creativity and abundance, and the still, quiet voice of intuition is a close friend, easily accessed at any time. You begin to embody reverence, and all of your life feels whole and complete.

> *Showing up reverently requires first connecting to yourself and your story and being willing to remove or change anything that stands between you and what you feel called to do.*

The upper level stages of reverence include the gifts of your true essence from spirit: love, joy, and peace. Almost everyone experiences these states at some point. Some only receive a glimpse, but with practice, you can cultivate these higher states for long periods.

In these states, everything seems to move more slowly, like a movie being played in slow motion. You live in the present moment. Your mind is not overtaken by thoughts of the past or worry about the future. You are right here, right now, in the now, celebrating all the beauty without the baggage of a past or attachment to your sad story.

As a young girl, I remember feeling states of peace, love, and joy when I went for a long walk on our property. I imagined I was a Native American, and I would place intention on walking more slowly, feeling how my feet touched the ground with each step, hearing how the leaves crinkled, noticing every sound around me, focusing on my breath entering and leaving my nose as I walked and took in every sight and sound in the moment. I felt deeply connected with nature, and here I would release experiences that made me feel depleted.

I used visualization back then to imagine feeling loved and free.

I used to lie on my back on a big rock in a dried-up creek bed and look up at the sky, amazed at the beautiful, expansive universe. I imagined while looking up at a tree—that I was the tree and my branches reached up and swayed in the wind. I would sometimes saddle my horse Singer and gallop along the side of the long stretch of highway running past our property. I imagined I became the horse as we galloped together for miles. I felt free, joyful, and loved in these moments. Without realizing it, I was practicing a form of meditation, connecting with the power of the present moment and feeling the connection with nature and the gifts of reverence.

As I grew older, it wasn't until I began letting go of emotions and attachment to the disempowered perception of my story that I experienced the gifts of love, joy, and peace more often and more easily. Now I can embody these blissful states by simply making the choice to feel joy and gratitude, during deep prayer and meditation, in those peaceful moments with my children at bedtime, while guiding people through breakthroughs and powerful visualizations, during worship, and while speaking as an instrument for change. I still encounter challenges, and emotions still creep up, but I am now better equipped to turn them around quickly, rise up outside of the story, and honor the lessons they are bringing me. As you become willing to be unleashed into third story reverence, all that is necessary for your transformation will present itself.

Living in the Reverence stage of third story has a profound effect on the success of your relationships, your leadership style, your story style, and your ability to attract abundance. The following describes what it is like to live in third story in each of these areas.

RELATIONSHIP STYLE: Third Story, Reverence

Moving into third story creates a massive shift in relationships. Criticism turns into compassion. Expectations turn into altruism or selfless service to the other. Toxic relationships fall away. Relationships not aligned in reverence will begin to shift and either fall away or deepen. A deep love can be cultivated because there is a strong sense of self-love and selflessness in place. You begin to see your partner in a different way—not as someone who must fulfill a physical or material need, but rather as a partner who complements your already joyful life. You will experience a sense of peace in your relationship, and the reverence you will experience comes from the recognition that somehow you selected one another to be partners on this journey.

Immense gratitude comes over you, and the epiphany in third story is that being in a relationship is no longer about you. The bigger picture is that this partner is the perfect companion to bring you to altruism and the experience of unconditional love. This also rings true for deep, meaningful friendships.

The epiphany in third story reverence is that being in a relationship is no longer about you. The bigger picture is that this partner is the perfect companion to bring you to altruism and the experience of unconditional love.

Whether you are in a relationship or not, unconditional love knows no bounds. It does not play by the rules that society has set, nor does it fit into a box. Reverent love lives at its highest frequency, unnamed and untamed. Love is an energy at work that erupts when two or more people share a common bond. This bond can be between friends, colleagues, and through the synergistic magic that occurs in a creative project. Spirit is the basis of this creativity. When you can tap into it, any relationship with a person or a creative project that is grounded in reverence for the process can manifest because it stems from the power of limitless possibilities.

LEADERSHIP STYLE: Third Story, Reverence

Reverent leaders have all the qualities of unleashed leaders. The difference is they see the big picture more clearly and view their work as a spiritual responsibility. Reverent leaders are more invested in their people. They realize their teams spend many hours away from their families, so they will typically create a family atmosphere for their businesses. Third story leaders feel called to give in some way. They may create non-profits or give proceeds from their businesses to charity. They are very generous with their teams. Since they are not operating in the ego state, it is natural for them to give of themselves and fully embody servant leadership.

Expressing gratitude for their teams and clients comes easily to them. Reverent leaders typically create a peaceful, joyful work environment, and they believe work/life balance is key to the fundamental motivation of their teams. Reverent leaders make decisions based on intuition, and typically, they are right when it comes to the best direction for their brand and team. Pure creativity becomes the driving force in reverent leadership. All voices, no matter their status, are encouraged to bring forth innovative ideas. Reverent leaders raise up other leaders.

STORY STYLE: Third Story, Reverence

Telling your story from reverence is a huge leap in consciousness. Your story is no longer about having overcome something. That's right. Your story is whole and perfect just as it is. You no longer see your story from the perspective of right or wrong. You realize everyone has played a part in the story of your life, helping you reach a reverent state. You sincerely feel gratitude for all of your story. You begin to develop a deep compassion for the people who played a role in the hurt and pain you've experienced—and for all humankind has experienced. Your intuition is at its highest state in third story, and you can feel where others are coming from. You easily reach states of bliss, and your creativity pours through you. You feel a sense of peace when you look back on your life.

Telling your story in this state, it may be difficult to connect to how you felt back then. You may even forget many of the details. Your life feels whole and complete. No matter how the journey unfolded, everything feels perfect. From a scientific perspective, you have created new neuropathways to memories that may have, in the past, triggered you back into disempowering states. You now have a different perspective of those memories, and you have wrapped your story in gratitude, love, and honor for self and all the participants of your story. While telling your story in third story reverence, it may be impossible not to smile, and crying tears of gratitude and joy is common. In your writing and any other means by which you express your story and creativity, gratitude pours through you. You are able to rise above your story fully and tell it from a purely conscious state. You are ultimately connected to spirit, where all creativity and inspiration flows.

Telling your story from reverence is a huge leap in consciousness. Your story is no longer about having overcome something. That's right. Your story is whole and perfect just as it is.

ABUNDANCE: Third Story, Reverence

In third story reverence, you are in the ultimate flow of abundance. You have no attachment to money, and it becomes much easier to attract it. You may feel the need to get rid of excess material things, and it is natural to want to give and be generous with others. As you look around, you feel at peace just by the loving, authentic relationships you have. You feel whole and complete, and you don't need anything outside of yourself to feel joy. You feel joyful because your life's currency is not based in the physical world. You have shifted to seeing everything from a reverent perspective. You realize that everything you intend can create a ripple effect. You feel inclined to make a positive change using your gifts and talents, and you feel a sense of connectedness to all life, seen and unseen. You are tapped into ultimate intuition and pure creativity—this is the source of the freedom you exemplify.

REVERENCE EXERCISE:

Taking 100 percent of the responsibility for how you participated in your own story can create a massive shift into reverence. As a young child, you were responding within the awareness of a child. Now, as an adult, you can respond with a reverent awareness of the big picture of your story. As you begin to accept responsibility for your story and you monitor and shift both your perception and emotions, you are gifted with the ability to see the rich lessons weaved within your story and can wrap it all in reverence.

The Ho'oponopono prayer, used by Dr. Ihaleakala Hew Len to help heal patients in a psychiatric ward in Hawaii, is a powerful exercise in shifting into reverence of your story: "I love you. I'm sorry. Please forgive me. Thank you." He believes that anything in your life, whether you had control over it or not, is your responsibility. To change your life, you have to change yourself. This prayer activates reverent awareness within yourself. Cited over and over, it can help you shift into compassion and gratitude, the basis of reverence.

In third story reverence, you are in the ultimate flow of abundance. You feel whole and complete, and you don't need anything outside of yourself to feel joy. You feel joyful because your life's currency is not based in the physical world.

SHIFTING YOUR STORY TO COMPASSION AND GRATITUDE:

Below, write a few sentences about your story and your responsibility in it. Write out statements that bring compassion to yourself and others surrounding this story. Then write the lesson(s) you can now take with you about this story and your gratitude statements. Anytime you feel triggered, whether it be big or small, you can do this exercise to shift your perception of your story to compassion and gratitude.

Story:

_____

_____

_____

_____

_____

_____

Responsibility:

_____

_____

_____

_____

_____

Compassion statements:

_____

_____

_____

_____

_____

Lesson(s):

_____

_____

_____

_____

_____

_____

Gratitude statements:

_____

_____

_____

_____

_____

_____

Story:

_____

_____

_____

_____

_____

_____

Responsibility:

_____

_____

_____

_____

_____

_____

Compassion statements:

_____

_____

_____

_____

_____

_____

Lesson(s):

_____

_____

_____

_____

_____

_____

Gratitude statements:

_____

_____

_____

_____

_____

Now scan each story and wrap them all in reverence.

INVITATION:

I invite you to download the color chart: *Your Story of Intention* from UnleashYourRising.com/resources and post it in your home, on your refrigerator, by your vision board, and in your work area. Anytime you experience disempowering states, ask yourself:

What is required of me to unleash into a higher level of intention? Follow the 1. Acknowledge, 2. Release, 3. Intend (ARI) steps to rise up.

Awareness of *Your Story of Intention* and incorporating the ARI steps can profoundly change your relationships, your ability to lead, the way you embody your story, and your ability to attract abundance.

CHAPTER 5

Listening to the Still, Quiet Voice

*I am a dreamer who dreams, sees visions, and listens always
to the still, small voice. I am the trail blazer.*

— GEORGE WASHINGTON CARVER

When I lived in Philadelphia, I was working for a corporation
making a high, executive salary, when I began wondering, "Is this
all there is?" I had stopped going out on the weekends, and instead,
I would stay home with my cat Biscuit, drink a glass of red wine,
and go to bed early. By Monday, I would feel resistance to going
to work even though I was the company's top-performing account
executive and doing very well financially. Inside, I felt empty and
asked, "What is my purpose?" "What is next for me?" I had asked
myself these questions before, but this time I began to listen.

When I say listen, I mean I started to tune in to the still, quiet voice
from within that answers when you ask yourself a question. It is not
an audible voice. Rather, it is a still, quiet knowing. It has a voice,
but it speaks from within.

One of the first times I heard this voice was three years prior to
completing my teaching certification. I was teaching my practi-

cum in English in the ninth and eleventh grades at a high school
in Southern New Jersey. I was also contemplating an opportunity
to become a teaching assistant at Rutgers University while working
toward my master's and doctorate to become an English professor.
This was definitely a crossroads for me. As one of eight children, I
had managed to put myself through college with the help of living
with the Ugoletti family as a part-time nanny and working various
jobs to make ends meet. Now I found myself pondering what I was
going to do with my life.

I planned an independent study abroad to Europe to study
Shakespeare and the architecture of castles. Everyone thought I was
crazy going to Europe alone, but while lying on the grass by the Eiffel
Tower's fountains, I began journaling and mapping out my life. The
still, quiet voice was crystal clear: "You are meant to reach youth and
people in a more meaningful way." I heard it again standing at the
top of the steps at Rutgers University one week before graduation. It
came over me, the knowing that I would live in California. Then the
still, quiet voice said, "Not yet." I asked why, and the answer came
back that I needed to make money and get some work experience.
So I did.

The still, quiet voice was crystal clear: "You are meant to reach youth and people in a more meaningful way."

I went out and joined the proverbial rat race, making six figures within
the first year of graduating. Two years later, the voice pushed me to
dive into my spirituality, so I found a faith I resonated with, and

within a few weeks of receiving a spiritual cleansing and a new start through baptism, the voice said: "Give the wine a break, take coffee and sugar out of your diet, and move back home." It became obvious that, although I had visited my family every year over the past twelve years, it was time to move back and reconnect with my roots in Texas. I had moved away when I was only eighteen, and now at thirty, I intended to move back to be near my family, buy a home, continue to build my financial success, and eventually adopt children.

My plan to never marry backfired because the first week back in Texas, I met Chris, and after numerous group dates with friends, we both knew we were destined for one another. The events that ensued included embarking on a deeper spiritual journey. I found I could experience peace throughout the day if I focused on being present in the moment. I learned how to heal past traumas and began to live in the space of peace and quiet in my mind. As I faced difficult parts of my childhood, a door opened for the beginning stages of forgiveness. On top of getting really clear spiritually and health-wise, I was reading every book I could get my hands on, learning more about the body, mind, spirit, psychology, the power of intention, the Law of Attraction, and the brain.

I found I could experience peace throughout the day if I focused on being present in the moment. I learned how to heal past traumas and began to live in the space of peace and quiet in my mind. As I faced difficult parts of my childhood, a door opened for the beginning stages of forgiveness.

One night, after two years of living back home, I was woken at 3:38 a.m. by a dream. The still, quiet knowing pulled me out of bed. I wanted to go back to sleep, yet I felt pulled and was obedient when the still, quiet voice instructed me to write. Nope, not on my computer. The voice was clear: "Pen and paper." For the first time since I was a teenager, I put pen to paper and found myself furiously writing everything down that I saw in the dream.

In the dream, I was in a big room full of people, most sitting in chairs scattered all over the room. What I could gather from the dream is that I was helping people facilitate breakthroughs. It felt amazing.

When I was finished writing, I read it, over ten pages, and wondered what in the world it all meant. People were connecting through stories and sharing. It was beautiful. I had no idea at the time that I had received a vision of directing personal development events. I realize in hindsight I was given a glimpse of part of my purpose. That is something I really deserved to see because, deep down, I was feeling that Texas was a pit stop on this journey. This was God's way of giving me a glimpse of something in the future, so I could allow my purpose to unfold.

Chris and I began to receive clues that we would be moving. Philadelphia kept coming up, and I kept resisting because I truly wanted to be in California. I asked, "Why not California?" The answer again was, "Not yet." I still resisted because I had just left Philadelphia and I had no intention of going back. After a heated discussion with Chris about moving there, the next day, he received a phone call from a 215 number. He immediately called it back, and the number was disconnected! Two-one-five is a Philadelphia area code. That mysterious telephone call was the icing on the cake of all the other nudges we were receiving, directing us back to the City of Brotherly Love. We felt that, since I knew a lot of people in Philadelphia, it would be a great location for Chris to build his chiropractic business while I figured out what to do.

Moving to Philadelphia, we met amazing people, including a healing mentor for me who also developed a strong bond with our first daughter. Another would become a godmother to both our children. Within six months of moving to Philadelphia, it came to me, after reading Wayne Dyer's book, *The Power of Intention*, that part of my bigger vision was to help underprivileged youth. The only way I felt I could do that was to launch my own home-infusion company and build it to the point where I would have an overflow of abundance so I could give in that way. I had successfully built over $10 million in the industry, mostly ground up revenue for various companies, over six years prior. All it took for me was to build a plan, find a clinical partner, and go for it. Within a few months, I branded all the materials, found a clinical partner, and was leading all of my company's sales and business operations. We got off to a slower start than expected, then gained momentum in the second year.

I got pregnant and began wondering whether Philadelphia was where we wanted to raise our family. We lived in an affluent area called The Mainline and had a wonderful group of friends. My husband's business was growing. However, when we began considering where we wanted to raise our family, Philadelphia didn't feel right. The still, quiet voice said, "No, this likely isn't it." Really? Weren't we sent here through a mysterious phone call? What now? We begrudgingly began to open our hearts for the answer.

Someone told us about a one-day event in New York where we could meet Wayne Dyer. We bought tickets right away and drove up that weekend. With my copy of *The Power of Intention* in hand, I listened intently as Dr. Dyer spoke about how we can live a life of intention and align with our deeper purpose. Dyer was one of the authors I listened to while driving around all day in my work. Listening to Dyer in person, in the flesh, was profoundly different and an experience I considered an invitation from God to respond to the call of my higher self. I was able to hear Dyer's stories and absorb his energy, intention, and every word in person.

I realized that, while I had the intention to do something meaningful, I kept chasing money that had historically come easily in the medical services industry. Something was missing. Although I owned my company and, through our services, we were making a positive impact on people's health, I was still in an industry that didn't reach people on a deeper level. I asked myself while sitting there, "Why am I here?"

The still, quiet voice told me to keep doing what I was doing for now and find happiness doing it. I placed my hand over my belly where my little girl, just five months in vitro, was growing happily and healthily. At that moment, Dyer began telling the story of a Norwegian opera singer named Cecilia. He played her beautiful rendition of "Amazing Grace" with the sound of dolphins in the background. I felt this song permeate my body. I felt a knowing in that moment that I would name my daughter Grace.

I kept my hand over my belly and infused my intention of love into her. I knew then that every decision I would make from now on would be equally guided by her purpose and where she was meant to be. I felt, listening to the dolphin sounds, that I would eventually live in California.

When I walked up to the stage to meet Wayne, I never told him I was pregnant. He looked up intently with his piercing blue eyes and said, "God bless you. God bless you." He said it twice, just like that. I left wondering if he instinctively knew I was carrying a child or if he meant me and my husband. I decided it meant both.

I felt I was exactly where I was supposed to be, and it was leading me to something greater.

After the event, I felt I was exactly where I was supposed to be, and it was leading me to something greater. Returning to work, I began to infuse the intention that everything I did would lead to something greater into my work and also fulfill my children's purposes. Four and a half months later, Grace was born, almost two weeks past her due date. After thirty-two hours of hypnobirthing, I wouldn't dilate past five centimeters. I breathed through each and every contraction while our dear friend Robbie held my hand and Chris cried by my side. My labor slowed down after dry heaving and receiving IV hydration.

I remember the doctor coming in to tell me, despite my daughter maintaining a strong heartbeat, that my body was not cooperating, and we should consider a C-section. Despite the sadness I felt because my body had failed me, the still, quiet voice told me it was time we bring her into this world and that everything was going to be okay. I felt a quiet peace come over me as I surrendered to the outcome. Fifteen minutes later, they cut me open and our beautiful Grace entered the world. The first time I laid eyes on her, I felt utter bliss and ecstasy. A feeling of intense, unconditional love I had never experienced before in all my life came over me. Our bond was instantaneous, and I knew we were meant to be together. My life had never felt so joyful.

As Grace reached the age of two, my company reached over $3 million total in topline revenue. Collecting on outstanding receivables, we would start to make money in our fourth year. We had a great team, and I felt accomplished for competing in a saturated market. Other than the heartfelt accomplishments of fighting through the FDA & USDA red tape to be the first home infusion company in Philadelphia to provide a life-saving therapy for a miraculous little girl just one week older than Grace, providing inotropic therapy for people awaiting heart transplants, and the wonderful friendships I made through clients, there was still a deeper calling pulling me. I couldn't describe it, and I had no idea what it was. I remembered how, at the Dyer event, I felt I was exactly where I was supposed to be. Now, after battling with my business partner for six months, it became apparent my partner intended to keep our company small. I realized that considering our high overhead, if my partner was not willing to expand more, I would never realize my dream to live in abundance and have an overflow to bless others. On top of that, I kept asking myself, "What about California? Remember that still, quiet voice? When are we ever going to get there?"

It became very clear it was time for me to walk away from my company I had put my heart and soul into. I felt an intense sadness along with a quiet knowing that letting go was the right thing to do. This time, the still, quiet voice spoke to my husband, and to our surprise, we found out that the second home on his Iowa family farm was going to be available if we wanted to take it. The family who had lived there for over twenty-five years was moving out. Iowa was miles away from California, but at least it was the halfway mark across the country. With Grace being only two, we realized this was a beautiful opportunity for her and my husband to connect with his family. After weeks of contemplation and opening our hearts for direction, I walked away from the partnership. When I did, I felt immense freedom.

> *It became very clear it was time for me to walk away from my company I had put my heart and soul into. I felt an intense sadness along with a quiet knowing that letting go was the right thing to do.*

This turning point was when I felt for the first time I could become a coach; however, I had no idea how to start. One thing was certain—I felt deep love and beautifully, intrinsically rewarded by being Grace's mother. It was a time to bask in that love, to take in all the simplicity of living on the family farm, which had been passed down for five generations, in the middle of nowhere in Iowa. It was exactly what I needed to grieve the loss of the dream I had for my company and just simply be.

After a year of diving into farm life, remodeling the old farmhouse, and Grace developing a beautiful connection with Chris' side of the

family, we began seeing signs that Iowa was not our final destination. We had decorated Grace's room with a beach scene, and every
night she would ask me to tell her a story about having a picnic
on the beach and walking along the seashore picking up beautiful
seashells like the ones attached to the top of her walls. At that point,
I had taken a job out of necessity and boredom and was driving over
four hours round trip just to go to work. Grace was dropped off at
daycare at six-thirty in the morning and picked up after four o'clock
every day. This wasn't the life we had planned.

I realized that something had to change. One day in December,
when I made the two-hour drive to Des Moines for work, it began
snowing really hard mid-day. I left to make the two-hour drive back
to pick up Grace from daycare. We had had bucket loads of snow a
few days prior, and in Iowa, the snow didn't go away…it just piled
up. The snow was coming down fast on my way back. I picked
up Grace in town, then drove to our farmhouse. I turned in on
our half-mile-long driveway and realized it had snowed quite a bit
since I had left that morning and the wind had blown an additional
foot of snow across the driveway. I slid around on the way up the
driveway, and my SUV ended up in the ditch. We were stuck. I got
out and looked at the half-mile-long driveway ahead of me. So this
was why Chris' father and brother had always said, "I don't know
why anyone would want to live in that old farmhouse—it has such
a long driveway!"

I had a work bag with my laptop in it, two bags full of groceries I
had picked up in Des Moines at Whole Foods, and Grace. She was
crying. I cursed to myself and somehow managed to carry her, the
groceries, and my laptop bag through two feet of snow in high-

heeled boots and a dress skirt all the way up this long, snow-filled driveway. With tears pouring down both our faces, I wondered, *How in the world did I get into this mess?* I felt the grief of leaving my business come up, and I allowed it. I allowed every ounce of it, and I felt the release, little by little, with each foot dragging through the snow, as I let go. I began to feel stronger and lighter.

I began laughing!

Then it came to me: Wow, here I was. I had grown a multi-million-dollar company only to give it up and live in twenty-below-zero weather on a big farm in the middle of nowhere. As I trudged up the driveway, I continued to laugh and Grace laughed with me.

My grief turned to appreciation. Appreciation for everything! I said to my daughter, "Grace, I love Iowa; don't you? This is great! We got stuck in the snow, and we get to live to tell this story; isn't that great?" She said, "I love you, Mommy. I could have walked!" We laughed as I picked up speed and reached the front door.

I felt free!

All of a sudden, the same knowing came over me that I had experienced standing on the campus center steps at Rutgers University after my last class before graduation. *I will be living in California.* This time, the message was clear: *soon.* It was like God was telling me, "You are getting closer, Christine. Just be patient. You needed the pit stop to connect with Chris' family, to release the business, and so I can prepare you for what I have for you." I spent the next few months continuing to make that trip to Des Moines and back for work. I gave my work my all, and I had gratitude for it, knowing something would change soon.

Then it came to me: Wow, here I was. I had grown a multi-million-dollar company only to give it up and live in twenty-below-zero weather on a big farm in the middle of nowhere. As I trudged up the driveway, I continued to laugh and Grace laughed with me. My grief turned to appreciation.

The week of Christmas, something popped up on my computer about chiropractic practices for sale. When I searched California, a practice in the San Diego suburbs came up. We knew we were being directed again to listen and trust. Not long afterwards, the company I was working for announced management positions opening up all over the country. I jumped on the opportunity for the branch in Northern California, and within weeks, I accepted the position. Finally, the knowing I had experienced on the steps of Rutgers University twelve years prior was coming to fruition. After all these years of knowing California was where I would eventually call home, this company was paying for our entire cross-country move. Talk about manifestation and divine provision! As we solidified plans for the move, we found out I was pregnant again. It was difficult to leave Chris' family, yet we knew we were meant to move to California. I received a huge promotion, a brand-new challenge with a new branch, and it seemed everything was in perfect alignment. I dove into my new position, while equally questioning how in the world I would keep up the pace after my second daughter was born. The still, quiet voice whispered to me, "It will all work out. The answer will come."

Five months later, I received that answer; however, it was not at all what I had expected or prepared for. My office received news of company layoffs and branch closings across the country, including our branch. The closing was a shock and Chris had not obtained his chiropractic license yet.

I learned quickly the true power of surrender, not only when we received the surprising news that left me jobless just a month before my due date, but even more so the night Elizabeth came into the world. Labor hit fast and hard. Within an hour, we were at the hospital; an hour later, the staff could not detect a heartbeat. As they called *code blue*, I immediately felt a rush of panic, and just as quickly, I prayed, "I surrender this outcome to you." They left Chris in the main delivery room as they swiftly wheeled me into surgery. I had no idea if he would be joining us. My panic lifted as I surrendered the outcome. A peaceful knowing came over me that everything was going to be okay. I just kept sending my unborn daughter love as they wheeled me under the blinding lights, and the medical personnel hustled around me to prep. Just as the surgeon went in to cut, Chris appeared by my side, holding my hand, looking deep into my eyes. We knew all we could do is surrender the outcome. Elizabeth was delivered via emergency C-section. I felt an even deeper peace as she was placed on my chest and we bonded right away. I wondered how we could be so blessed to have two healthy happy children when others struggle to conceive or have children with medical challenges. I sent them all love and peace.

The next morning, I witnessed the most beautiful sight: the first time Grace laid her eyes on Elizabeth and held her in her arms. Grace had already named Elizabeth when she was just two months in vitro. She had told me matter-of-factly at just three years old, "The little baby growing in your belly is my sister. Her name is Elizabeth. Right now, she lives far, far away, and we haven't seen each other in a long time. When she is born, we will be together again." There was no arguing with her about the name. When Grace arrived at the hospital to meet her sister, we had just confirmed with the nurse that her name would be Elizabeth. I have never seen Grace so happy. The four of us went home with joy in our hearts and a feeling that our family was complete.

> *I learned quickly the true power of surrender, not only when we received the surprising news that left me jobless just a month before my due date, but even more so the night Elizabeth came into the world . . . . As they called code blue, I immediately felt a rush of panic, and just as quickly, I prayed, "I surrender this outcome to you."*

After a few days, the discomfort set in because we had no idea how we were going to provide for our family past my six-month severance. Chris applied for his chiropractic license, and we continued to surrender and allow what was meant for us to unfold. At this point, it seemed the still, quiet voice was too quiet. In fact, I couldn't hear it at all. I had a three-year-old and a newborn. We had no family there for support. I had a rough C-section recovery and three bouts of mastitis. I felt alone despite having a beautiful family. I was tired of trusting in a company to provide for our family, and I was ready to step into what was meant for me. I was tired of moving all over the place. We both just wanted to feel like where we were living was home and we had the security to move forward. Yet the voice was still quiet.

Then one morning, I woke up to a realization. Grace was by my side. Elizabeth was breastfeeding. I announced that we were buying the practice in San Diego. Why would we stay in Northern California and wait around for me to get on my feet? It was Chris' turn to steer the ship. We reached out to the owner of the practice in San Diego we had researched more than a year prior. I realized the voice was quiet because everything that was meant for us was already there. We just had to rise into it. The still, quiet voice was waiting on us to take the action.

> *I realized the voice was quiet because everything that was meant for us was already there. We just had to rise into it. The still, quiet voice was waiting on us to take the action.*

I spent the next year enjoying both of my girls while daydreaming about the kind of career change I would be making. What looked like a ping-pong match all over the country was truly a journey to bring us exactly where we were meant to be, in this exact space and time. Everything was in divine alignment as we bought the practice and got settled in San Diego. It felt like we had at last found our home in Southern California. Within two years, after attending Oprah's Super Soul Sessions in Los Angeles, I found myself in the momentum of writing this book, building my coaching and speaking platform, and attracting mentors who continue to inspire me to stand in this message. My connection with the still, quiet voice continues to grow to this day, and it serves as my divine guidance system. The more in tune I become with it, the more often it speaks to me.

HONORING YOUR STILL, QUIET VOICE:

By accessing your still, quiet voice, you are accessing your unconscious mind. Some may call it their higher self or soul. I personally refer to it as my intuition or God speaking to me. What matters is that you practice listening and honoring it. You'll know it is your intuition rather than your ego because it gives you peace rather than stress. It is a still, quiet, peaceful voice, and it always answers in short, simple sentences. To truly step into effective self-leadership, I invite you to be in integrity with the still, quiet voice that guides you when you ask a question. Some may not understand what this means. They may say they don't hear anything when they ask a question. Typically, that is because they are solely in their conscious brain. They may hear something come back that is critical, suspecting, or all over the place. That is their inner critic yapping away. Listening to the still, quiet voice takes practice. You can practice by asking simple questions like: "Does this food serve my higher good?" "What is the best response to choose here?" "Am I living in my purpose?" You can further strengthen your ability to listen by taking good care of your health and practicing clearing the mental clutter through prayer, mindfulness, or meditation so you are in a space where you can listen.

Where have you heard the still, quiet voice in your life? Have you taken action to follow through with what it asks of you? Journal your responses here:

_____

_____

_____

_____

_____

_____

_____

Ask yourself these sample questions to exercise your ability to hear the still, quiet voice. When you implement the nudges you receive, your life will begin to change.

What was I sent here to do?

Am I living at my greatest potential?

Is this relationship good for me?

How can I shift to compassion and gratitude in my relationship to ignite more love?

What lesson was I meant to learn from a difficult part of my life?

How can I tap into my creativity?

Where is the best place for me to live?

Am I honoring my gifts and talents?

What time should I go to bed?

What exercise regime can I implement to honor my health?

What foods best honor my body?

What is the next inspired action step in my life?

What changes can I make as a leader?

What can I do differently to live in a more joyful state?

CHAPTER 6

Rising Into Your Voice and the Bigger Picture of Your Life

The one thing that you have that nobody else has is you. Your voice, your mind, your story, your vision. So write and draw and build and play and dance and live as only you can.

— NEIL GAIMAN

As you open yourself to the answers that come when you ask how to step into your voice and the bigger picture of your life, you may be gifted with opportunities to step out of your comfort zone. People may show up as healers, coaches, or teachers. Embrace them! When the student is ready, the teacher will come. When I work with clients, I find that much of the paralyzed will keeping them from finding their voices goes back to their childhoods. There is usually a story of an adult, typically a parent, overly asserting their beliefs and, unaware in their own unconscious state, shutting the child down. Some people choose careers that serve the desires of society or their family and find later that their creative voice became lost. You may still feel triggered by aspects of your story. It may creep up on you when you least expect it. Embrace it! If you are triggered, it is a mirror of something that still requires release. If you are willing to stand in the darkness of yourself, become unleashed into your voice, and wrap those parts of yourself and your story in light, love, and forgiveness, you will feel free. You will begin to feel peace and become conscious of how that part of your life served your greater purpose.

> *If you are willing to stand in the darkness of yourself, become unleashed into your voice, and wrap those parts of yourself and your story in light, love, and forgiveness, you will feel free.*

It was Christmas Eve at our home in San Diego. We had just returned from a beautiful choir Mass and our Feast of the Seven Fishes dinner. We all changed into our Christmas Eve pajamas. The girls were excited as we lit a pumpkin spice candle and put on our favorite Christmas music. I picked up my three-year-old daughter, and together, we admired the beautiful tree, lit with white lights and adorned with ornaments that signified our life. I entered into a beautiful, blissful state of gratitude for the true meaning of Christmas and for my family. At the same time, I felt a sadness over the Christmases I didn't have as a child—grief hanging out in the background of my bliss. I was surprised I could feel the bliss and still feel the sadness.

Then I remembered the revelation I'd had at seventeen, standing on stage, acting out the grief of a mother who had lost her child and peering out into the audience, feeling their hearts opening up with love. I remembered that on the other side of grief lies a deeper understanding of love. I was standing in that love, yet still experiencing grief.

We celebrated Christmas the next day, and just like every year, I woke up the next morning and had no voice. Christmas night I had experienced a severe scratchiness in my throat, like a cat was scratching it out. I could feel my throat energy area spinning a thousand miles per hour. This was all accompanied by a tightening, like someone was squeezing my throat. I knew this all too well, as every holiday season as a child, I would get strept throat. Then, as I got healthier and into my adult life, around the holidays I would lose my voice. This was an emotional response to my grief. Two weeks went by and I was still battling this loss of voice as I took all the lights and ornaments off the tree. Yet another Christmas went by, and I was still processing grief from my childhood. It was time to let this go once and for all.

I declared to my coach, Megan Unsworth, "I am placing firm intention on not losing my voice next Christmas." That night, I declared the same to my husband. During this time, I was asking God to download information and inspiration, and to give me guidance in writing this book to allow the message to flow through me onto the page. I didn't realize that in asking for this gift, I was also asking for clarity for my continued healing.

The following morning, my three-year-old daughter Elizabeth crawled into bed with me around 4 a.m. By quarter to five, I realized the little wiggle worm was going to keep me awake, so I decided to move to the couch. I hit snooze when my cellphone alarm went off at five-thirty and fell into a dream about my father. We were in a verbal altercation. I began to yell, but nothing came out. I was trying to yell to express my anger, but something was caught in my throat. I reached into my throat and began pulling out a stretchy playdough-like material. It just kept coming and coming out of the depths of my throat, and I kept pulling and pulling it out. I felt disempowered, unable to express myself and have my voice heard. When my alarm went off again, I woke to the realization that the source of my disempowerment was anger toward my father for abandoning our family's beliefs and traditions, and not fighting to keep these joyful celebrations alive for our family or allowing us to participate in what we felt passionate about.

I woke up determined that this was no longer going to take over my life! I had to switch this around. I thought I had already forgiven my parents. I had a wonderful relationship with them now after all these years. Yet there were still things left unhealed. I had not fully wrapped this story in forgiveness so my true voice could be fully expressed. I woke up angry at myself for allowing this to debilitate me. "Why can't I get over this already?" I asked myself. Have you ever felt this way?

Just a few weeks later, I went to a four-day leadership event focusing on abundance. I knew going in that I had a big breakthrough coming, and it was going to take more than the tools I knew and used to make it happen. It was going to take a community. I was very apprehensive. I knew the emotions I felt rising within affected my ability to connect deeply with people, so this was definitely outside of my comfort zone. When I arrived, the energy was amazing—full of love and excitement. Seventy people were there. I was terrified the release wouldn't work. I questioned whether this group could help me with a breakthrough to heal an issue from my childhood.

After two days of being there for other people's breakthroughs, I was definitely ready. For the third day, we were asked to bring a symbol of something that signified a part of our life we were ready to let go of. My first thought was to bring a symbol of the company I had owned and walked away from four years prior. That had been one of the most difficult decisions I had ever made. Then I asked myself about the cause of that partnership falling apart, and I realized I had never had the courage to stand up to my partners. I knew that my lack of courage had originated in my childhood.

I thought, *I am ready to take back my voice. I am ready once and for all to be vulnerable, speak the truth, and allow people in. I am ready to peel away this last layer of forgiveness so I can leave this anger and disempowerment behind once and for all.*

I had never had the courage to stand up to my parents and speak my truth. In that moment, I realized losing my voice every Christmas had everything to do with losing my voice as a child. It went beyond not celebrating Christmas. It included not being allowed to have friends and participate in activities. That was why it was going to take a community to heal it. I had spent my whole life yearning to be accepted and to express my creative gifts. Back then, I wanted to scream, "This isn't right!" The years and years of overly strict upbringing had finally accumulated and expressed themselves every Christmas in losing my voice. I was ready to get to the root of it all.

As I turned onto my street that evening, I thought, *I need a really big symbol that goes back to my childhood. Skip the business symbol. This goes way deeper. I am ready to take back my voice. I am ready once and for all to be vulnerable, speak the truth, and allow people in. I am ready to peel away this last layer of forgiveness so I can leave this anger and disempowerment behind once and for all.*

As I drove into our driveway on January 19, I saw it—the perfect symbol. There lay our seven-foot-tall Christmas tree, dead and shriveled up on the side of our yard. *This is it. I am going to burn this tree!* I told myself. This tree symbolized my life while burdened by the grief and loss of my childhood. I had gazed at that tree holding my Elizabeth. It had been lit up beautifully. I felt the magic of Christmas, the peace and gratitude for Christ's unconditional love. Equally, I felt sadness and grief for the loss of my childhood. It was time to let this go.

The next morning, I shoved that big tree into the back of my SUV and drove to the event venue shaking. My body was aware there was going to be a big release, and it was resisting. My mind was telling me, *I don't think this is going to work. What if this doesn't work?* My ego was holding on to this suppression and anger so tightly it made my body shake. When I arrived at the event, the same high calibration of love was present. I hugged a good friend and shook with fear and anticipation.

This is a perfect example of what it takes to move past fear. You have to stand in your fear. I stood in it all day until it was time to present our symbols. We then took a break and I left alone, leaving the building and going to my SUV, which was parked all the way at the back of the parking lot—at least a football field away. I opened the back and saw the tree lying there. I dragged it out and felt an overwhelming feeling of empowerment. As I carried this heavy, bulky tree back to the event, I yelled aloud, "I am not going to allow you to control me anymore. I am going to experience 100 percent peace, love, and joy every holiday from now on. I am claiming my voice back! I am done feeling grief over my childhood, and I am done yearning for acceptance. I am taking my life back! I trust in this community. This is going to work, dammit! I deserve to move on with my life!"

Anyone witnessing this scene would have likely thought I had lost my mind. I had. I was willing to lose this part of my mind—the part attached to this story of my upbringing. I was going to burn it all!

I opened the door. There everyone sat, staring blankly at me as I struggled to carry in a dead, seven-foot tree. People asked if I needed help. "No, thank you," I said as I stood in the back of the room holding this tree, tears streaming down my face. I was still shaking. I realized how ridiculous I must look, but I didn't care. Someone in the group said aloud, "This symbol must be a big one." We all laughed a bit. I laughed and cried at the same time.

I loved these people.

I felt the shift happening. I trusted the process, and I was so ready. Everyone had a chance to come up, talk about their symbol, and put it into the large trashcan. I realized most of the symbols represented times when they felt they did not show up as their true selves. They were ready to be unleashed from this experience and rise into their full potential, leaving this symbol of their past behind. I was moved by all of the breakthroughs, which took a great deal of pressure off my breakthrough.

I felt the shift happening. I trusted the process, and I was so ready.

When my turn came, I wrestled the tree over to the trashcan and stood with it, talking through tears about what this symbol meant to me, why I was ready to let it go, and how grateful I was for the experience. When I wrapped this experience of suppression in gratitude, I felt a release and a relief.

The trainer took the tree for me and put it outside. That evening I invited whoever wanted to join me to come to the beach to burn the tree in a bonfire pit. I knew burning the tree was important for completely closing this chapter in my life, but I had no expectation anyone would be there. After dinner, I found the largest pit on the beach and waited for the others to arrive. I couldn't have picked a colder, windier night!

My friends showed up.

We gathered around the pit in the freezing cold. I announced, "I am burning this tree to release the grief and suppression from my childhood. This is not just for me. This is for my sisters and brother who were affected by this situation as well. This is to help them heal that part of their lives so they can stand in their purpose and get their voices back. This is also for everyone else in the world who has experienced disempowerment or was unable to live in their true voice. I believe that in healing something within ourselves, we heal it for the world."

As I stared at the burning tree and watched it dwindle down to sizzling, bright-white coals, I imagined the ashes swirling around like a tornado around the fire pit until the tornado turned into a bright, white light. I sent my light into the swirling tornado, and each person standing there with me sent their light into it, and together, we wrapped that childhood story in love, compassion, and gratitude. I then visualized cutting the imaginary cord of disempowering attachment to this story, and wrapping all the experiences of losing my voice and all the experiences of disempowerment in my life into a bright-white tornado of light, love, and forgiveness.

I believe that in healing something within ourselves, we heal it for the world.

While this was happening, I felt my throat open. It was like that part in Disney's *The Little Mermaid* when Ariel's voice is restored. I imagined the swirl of light and love surrounding me, and from the ground up, it swirled around my body and entered into my throat. I got my voice back.

Never again would that ghost story from my past take over my life. I was restored in peace and love, and I felt the most incredible joy come over me. As the tree went up in flames, we all felt freedom, and I realized that in faith and in letting go, our innermost beingness of joy can rise up further. In this state, our inner child is expressed. We laugh more, we connect more, and we shift to become an instrument for others' transformations.

In faith and in letting go, our innermost beingness of joy can rise up further. In this state, our inner child is expressed. We laugh more, we connect more, and we shift to become an instrument for others' transformations.

BURNING A SYMBOL OF YOUR PAST:

Burning a symbol from your past can be the turning point in experiencing your life through third story reverence. I invite you to find a symbol from your past that represents part of your first story disempowerment and burn it. If you have friends or family who can join you in restoring peace and wrapping your grief story in light and love, it can heighten the experience to have the power of community. Either way, with community or alone, speak your truth aloud and give it all to God. You are never alone in this. Whomever you call upon for support, whether present or not, will be with you. I am also setting intention to support your release, wherever you are.

Journal about your symbol below.

Write about your story and what emotions the symbol represents.

_____

_____

_____

How did this symbol serve you in the past?

_____

_____

_____

What does this symbol signify for you now?

_____

_____

_____

Now, thank the symbol. "I am releasing this symbol _____ related to this time in my life _____ _____. This symbol served me by _____, and now, I no longer need it. I am grateful for _____ _____. I release the emotions of _____, _____, _____ attached to this symbol and wrap this ghost story from my past in light, love, forgiveness, peace, and gratitude."

Burn the symbol. If you cannot burn it, improvise whatever is necessary to let it go. Visualize this symbol, all that it represents, all the elements and people involved in this story, and wrap it all in a tornado of the bright, white light of forgiveness, peace, love, and gratitude. You can now stand outside of your story and see it with compassion and love. Embody reverence. Your story is whole and complete.

Embody reverence. Your story is whole and complete.

Journal about how this experience has restored you. How did you regain your voice? What have you risen above? How are you now free from this story?

_____

_____

_____

_____

_____

_____

_____

Everyone makes the best choices they can given their experiences, beliefs, and the information they know. How can you honor your journey and everyone's journey involved in this experience? What was the learning you can take with you now, to serve you in the present and the future?

_____

_____

_____

_____

_____

_____

How did it feel to wrap this experience in light, love, forgiveness, peace, and gratitude? How will your life be different now?

_____

_____

_____

_____

_____

_____

CHAPTER 7

Your Superpower of Intention and Language

Every action, thought, and feeling is preceded by intention.
Intention is the energy that infuses the deed or the word.
There are only two intentions...love or fear.

– GARY ZUKAV

INTENTION

The challenges and division we experience within and outside of ourselves are due to separation from the field of intention, the source of our aliveness. What if you could connect to this aliveness with deepened intuition and pure creativity, with a feeling of wholeness and completeness? You are made to experience the gifts of your true essence from spirit: peace, love, and joy. When you came into this world, you were celebrated and had all that you needed. What if you could feel celebrated and like you have all you need now? If you could take these gifts in gratitude and with compassion for all living things, and infuse them with reverent intention in all you do, every minute of your life would be magical. You would see your stories in a different way because you would honor every step of your journey as divine orchestration. You could then see your failures, pain, and challenges as opportunities for growth and the foundation of your strength. When the leaves on a tree turn red, orange, and yellow, and fall from the trees, this is not considered failure. Rather, it is rebirth in motion. As you embody reverence, you will experience rebirth and feel more deeply connected to the field of intention where ultimate intuition and pure creativity flow.

The challenges and division we experience within and outside of ourselves are due to separation from the field of intention, the source of our aliveness. What if you could connect to this aliveness with deepened intuition and pure creativity, with a feeling of wholeness and completeness?

Intention is also the energy behind all you do. Intention fuels the doing. The word intention is derived from the Latin word *intencio*, meaning "stretching, purpose." I found the root very interesting because within this book, you are learning to stretch yourself by igniting your story and honoring your reverent purpose. Just as outlined in the *Your Story of Intention* chapters, the story you are in determines your intention toward everything.

In the higher states of reverence, there is no attachment, and typically, the intention is for the greater good and to serve others. In this reverent state, while you may place intention on something, you are able to surrender to the process and be open to how it comes to you.

THE POWER OF LANGUAGE AND INTENTION

We manifest our intent through language. One powerful way to change what we manifest in our lives is by changing what we speak out loud. The saying goes, "Every thought is a prayer." Well, every spoken word is an even more powerful prayer. We can create our world through the power of our words. Having had an interest in language and words for many years, I began studying neuro-linguistic programming (NLP). NLP is the study of using the mind and language to bring about changes in habits, thoughts, feelings, and experiences.

I found that in changing my language, my eyes would open up larger, I felt more empowered, and I felt I was operating at a higher level of commitment. For example, rather than saying, "I am trying to write a book, but I don't have time," I began saying, "I am committed to writing my book, and I am carving out time regularly to honor the process. I get to write my book because I am standing as an instrument of a message bigger than me. I get to be a source of transformation for others." Rather than saying, "I need to make money," I said, "I deserve to attract money, and I can't wait to see how my life will flow with more ease when I do attract it."

I began replacing the word "need" with "deserve" on a regular basis. The word need comes from an intention of lack. The word deserve comes from an intention of empowerment. Someone told me once, "Christine, the world needs you." I responded with, "The world deserves me, and the world deserves you, too."

What about the "have tos" we all seem to have? "I have to do more videos to build my business." Notice how the energy of the task changes when you say, "I get to create more videos to build my business, and I can't wait to see the effect of inspiring more people." When you say, "I get to," you are automatically shifting from the intention of yearning and dissatisfaction found in first story disempowerment, to an intention of gratitude and serving found in third story reverence. Notice the shift in energy from a negative mindset in the statement, "I have to network," to a positive mindset in the statement, "I get to meet new people to expand my network and to support others in discovering how their story matters." Changing, "I can't afford that," or "That's too expensive," to "I am choosing to spend my money on other things," shifts from an intention of lack to an intention of empowerment through choice. Simply saying "I can" instead of "I can't" on a regular basis sets the intention that you can accomplish what you intend to do.

What about people who are programmed to say "no" all the time? When someone has a request of you, is it a default to automatically say "no"? Saying no to requests, invitations, and ideas shuts down the flow of intention, the possibility of being creative, and the opportunity to have a positive experience. When a member of your team suggests a change or has an idea, do you automatically respond with how it wouldn't work?

Walt Disney allowed anyone in any position to contribute ideas to the company. He believed that saying "no" was really an excuse not to think outside of the box. Consider responding with "yes, if" and allowing the collaboration to get to a yes to honor the input. This allows for the power of creativity to come forth in the state of reverent intention.

One powerful way to change what we manifest in our lives is by changing what we speak out loud.

HIDDEN MESSAGES IN WATER

Dr. Masuru Emoto, a Japanese scientist and water researcher, performed an in-depth study on the power of language and intention.

In research documented in his book *The Hidden Messages in Water*, he found that the human vibrational energy of thoughts, emotions, music, and the spoken word affect the molecular structure of water. In Japanese, the word "hado" means "vibration" or "wave motion." The word hado has been used in connection with the study of quantum physics. Quantum physics basically states that all things are in a state of vibration. Emoto showed that words and music carry a vibration that can be measured in water.

Using high-speed photography and a powerful microscope in a cold room, Dr. Emoto discovered that by exposing water to beautiful words and music and then freezing it, beautifully brilliant and complex snowflake-like crystals formed. When the water was exposed to negative, hateful words, the water did not crystalize and was malformed. An almost identical water formation occurred when playing heavy metal music as when the phrase "you fool" was taped onto a container of distilled water. Dr. Emoto tested tap water, water supplies near cities, and polluted water, finding they would not crystalize, but rather, their structure was dark and formless.

Free flowing water in nature showed beautiful crystal formations. The most beautiful crystals were formed by speaking the words "love" and "gratitude" over the water. Water particles collected from the Fujiwara Dam in Japan when frozen and observed under the microscope were dark and distorted. After one hour of prayer with the intention of fortune, the water crystalized to form a golden, seven-sided crystal, a heptagon, that Emoto had not observed in over 10,000 other water experiments.

Why are these water research discoveries so profound? Keep in mind that infants are made up of 70-75 percent water and adults are about

50-65 percent water. Our brains and hearts are 73 percent water, our lungs are a whopping 80 percent water, and our earth, itself, is comprised of 70 percent water. It is evident in Emoto's research that we can affect people or nature's cell structure in a negative or positive way just in the language we choose, through prayer, with music or intention.

We can affect people or nature's cell structure in a negative or positive way just in the language we choose, through prayer, with music or intention.

HEARTMATH RESEARCH

The HeartMath Institute in Boulder Creek, California, further developed intention and heart intelligence research, coining the term "coherence" for balanced physiological processes related to positive emotion. It further studied how "the heart's electromagnetic field can be detected by other individuals and can produce physiologically relevant effects in a person five feet away."

I was blown away by this research. For the first time, I understood how, when I felt I was in higher states of intention where unconditional love poured through me, I could send that intention through my heart to anyone, no matter where they were, and feel a connection. Sometimes that person would simultaneously send me a text message or call me. Then, as I began diving into the power of the Holy Spirit and the intention of healing, I wondered how all of this ties in scientifically? What physically happens in the body when we achieve heart coherence, in a positive, loving state, and infuse that with the intention to heal?

Dr. Glen Rein, a Harvard and Stanford biomedical researcher, believed that DNA was the best target for testing the effects of healers. He simply had the healers create a healing environment, then hold test tubes containing DNA. The DNA strands exhibited change.

Later, these three men—Doc Childre, HeartMath Institute founder; Dr. Rollin McCraty, HeartMath Institute Director of Research, also recognized for his research on heart rate variability, heart rhythm coherence, and the effects of positive and negative emotions on human psychophysiology; and Mike Atkinson, a co-holder of three patents related to physiological coherence monitoring used in organizational, educational, and healthcare settings—together further developed research to test the theory of heart intelligence infused with intention.

HeartMath participants were trained and tested on bringing themselves to positive emotional states resulting in highly balanced heart coherence. These trained HeartMath participants were divided into two groups. One of the groups would hold test tubes containing placental DNA and simply be in a positive emotional state of love and appreciation. The other group would do the same: Hold test tubes containing placental DNA, be in a positive emotional state of love and appreciation, and also place intention on either winding or unwinding the DNA. What they found was that the group that placed intention on altering the DNA strands and had the highest heart coherence saw the most significant change in the strands. Interestingly, these same participants were then instructed to no longer focus on heart coherence, but rather just place intention on changing the DNA. Just like the control group, the DNA strands showed no significant change. I find it interesting that although they placed intention on what they wanted, to change the DNA strands, since they had a normal heart coherence, no change occurred.

What they found was that the group that placed intention on altering the DNA strands and had the highest heart coherence saw the most significant change in the strands.

This immediately made me reconsider the long-standing idea of the Law of Attraction. The Law of Attraction states that by placing your intention on what you want, you can receive it. I always felt this concept was over-simplified and did not always work. The secret to the Law of Attraction is this—in addition to following through with intentional action steps, you must become a match vibrationally for what you want. This is why intention is so powerful. When you focus intention in the higher vibrational frequencies of love and appreciation and begin changing your belief systems to align with what you want, you can attract what you place your intention on. This is why some people who receive a cancer diagnosis can go into miraculous full remission just by practicing self-love, becoming more spiritually connected, placing intention on healing through prayer, writing letters to their disease, and releasing the disease through visualization. The same has been reported in healing and prayer groups. The overflow of love combined with the intention to heal creates miracles.

When you focus intention in the higher vibrational frequencies of love and appreciation and begin changing your belief systems to align with what you want, you can attract what you place your intention on.

Finally, scientific evidence is backing up what I have felt intuitively all along. The Law of Attraction goes so much deeper and has taken on a whole new dynamic. Research is confirming the notion that we can attract what we place intention on and our power rises when we are connected to our heart. By simply registering in the higher frequencies of third story reverence, you can more easily attract what you intend.

INTENTION OVER DISTANCE

When I discovered the power of intention infused with the higher vibrational frequency of love and connection, I began to test this in my work. At the time, I was back in the corporate medical services field after leaving my company. I spent most of my day driving around meeting with clients. While driving, I felt connected and would begin to download ideas. I felt as if I were invisibly aligned with what some call universal consciousness. The best way I can explain it is that I felt there was this database of information I could connect to that was running even when I was not connected. When I really paid attention, I could sense when to connect with specific clients. I found that when I was connected to this field of intention, I could sense when to follow up, and I knew when clients had business to give. As I dove into coaching and writing, I could tap into this database and receive information downloads. I could think of someone, and then they would reach out to me. I could speak something out loud, and days or weeks later, connect with someone who aligned with what I spoke.

You may be thinking this is purely coincidence. Have you ever had the experience where you were thinking of someone and then they called or texted you, or have you ever placed intention on something and received it? What is this invisible connection? How can you use intention over distance? What does science say about this?

At the HeartMath Institute, they decided to take the study on heart-focused intention a step further, testing it over a distance. What they discovered was astounding. A participant with high heart coherence half a mile away from the DNA test tube successfully caused a change in the DNA strand by just placing intention on the change. They also tested specific intentions by asking participants who were in high heart coherence to hold a test tube with three strands of DNA, put intention on one strand to wind tighter, one strand to unwind, and no intention on the third. The intentions the participants put on the DNA happened just as intended, and the third strand showed no change. Can you imagine the power we could have on our own bodies by simply being in a loving, appreciative state and placing intention on healing? This research explains, from a scientific perspective, the power behind group prayer, hands on healing, spontaneous remission in cancer, and mass meditation with the intention of love and peace for the world. This explains why, when we place intention on helping transform the world in some way, it changes. The foundation of this intention is love and compassion—with it, the wheels are set in motion for the shift to occur.

The power of heart-focused intention can literally change the composition of our DNA. We have the ability, with practice, either to create havoc or balance in our lives or in the world through our language, heart coherence, and intention. The combination of the three is your superpower.

CHAPTER 8

Letting Go

*Let go of your attachment to your past as an excuse for your life
conditions today. You are the product of the choices
you are making right now.*

— DR. WAYNE DYER

What would your life be like if you could let go of the stories that
hold you back and find more cause for celebration? Letting go can
be the most difficult part of transforming your life so that you can
become a stronger leader. What if you took 100 percent responsibility
for everything in your life and took 100 percent control of your story
from this point forward? What would change? According to Brian
Tracy, international speaker and best-selling author of *The Psychology
of Achievement*, we would be happier: "The happiest people in the
world are those who feel absolutely terrific about themselves, and this
is the natural outgrowth of accepting total responsibility for every
part of their life." What if we let go of trying to control how our story
is played out and instead change our perception to a willingness to
embrace all of the richness of our lives moment by moment?

Our brain works against us because we can typically recall painful memories more easily than joyful ones. For this reason, it is so

much easier for people to hold on to the sad stories of their lives. They create an emotional attachment to them and can recite them like a robot at the drop of a hat. Then they go through life carrying the weight of the emotions related to those stories, take action in the disempowerment stages, and wonder why the same story shows up over and over. Victims, deep down on an unconscious level, want their pain to be validated. They point the finger toward someone or something else as the cause of their pain. By doing this, they are unconsciously carrying around these stories as something that has happened to them, while seeking love, approval, and success from this space of lack. As long as they are pointing the finger toward someone or something they feel is wrong, rather than taking responsibility and changing their perception of it, this story will continue to play in the background, creating white noise that covers up their true essence of peace, forgiveness, unconditional love, and joyful celebration.

The other end of the spectrum is that they hold these stories inside to smolder and fester. They wouldn't dare share them with the world. Similarly, they are yearning outside of themselves for something to complete them and make up for their loss and grief. They may focus on elevating their intellectual knowledge and gaining material success, while they never really deal with the pain they have experienced. The latter used to be my predicament. I never spoke about my stories because they charged me emotionally, and I felt ashamed and different from everyone else. As I became aware that it was actually the emotions related to the stories I was holding on to, it became much easier to begin letting them go. In the letting go, I gained the strength to see the rich lessons in these stories, share my journey, and live in a deeper purpose. As I let go of the energy attached to these emotions that no longer served me, I could then be freed to use this energy toward my creative expression.

I want to encourage you today to stand in courage and face every instance of fear. If you do, you will feel free, you will feel more joyful, and you will feel empowered. The painful emotions attached to your stories can be released and wrapped in reverence. Go a step further and celebrate all of those stories as the source of your strength. Turn your pain into your power. This allows a door to open for attracting beautiful stories. You can literally transform the entire script of your life by letting go and finding what you can celebrate.

You can literally transform the entire script of your life by letting go and finding what you can celebrate.

EMOTIONS, STORIES, PERCEPTION, AND THE BODY

The most important thing to note about releasing emotions that do not serve you is realizing you are not your emotions. Emotions result from the stories you tell yourself about something that has happened. Emotions and stories are two different things, yet they can work very well together to craft a joyful script of your life or keep you from living the joyful life you deserve. You can craft a different script just by releasing emotions and changing your perception. Max Planck, a German physicist and Nobel Prize winner known as the founder of quantum physics, famously said, "When you change the way you look at things, the things you look at change." He demonstrated that an object's characteristics can actually change on a molecular level when an individual looks at it. The same goes for your story.

The first step to changing the perception of your story is to release the attached emotions that do not serve you. Sometimes it can be difficult to recognize the emotions and how you are feeling. This difficulty could be due to how you were raised. Some people were raised to believe that emotions are a weakness that must be covered up and never discussed. Emotions are a reaction to your perception of life events, and they can remain bottled up for years, stored in your body. What ends up happening is these people cover up emotions by watching hours of television, becoming addicted to sex or porn, playing video games, binge eating, binge shopping, drinking alcohol or doing drugs, constantly having to go do something to lift them up, calling a friend who will appease them and make them feel better on a surface level, becoming a workaholic, or just having to stay busy all of the time. Still, life will continue to present opportunities to let the emotions go.

Whether you realize it or not, the same stories will continue to play over and over. The emotions attached to these stories cause more stress and can manifest as disease. Research has proven that when traumatic emotions are released, health automatically improves.

YOU ARE READY AND STRONG

Life will present what you are ready and strong enough to let go of. How do you know? The emotions that carry the most intensity, where you cannot carry on a conversation or speak about them without crying or feeling angry, are the ones you are ready to release because they are presenting themselves to you right now. This presentation is a key indication that you are ready to let them go. Your body is signaling that it is time. It is important to understand that the stories we carry have a plethora of lessons weaved within them. As we clear out the cobwebs of painful emotions, we can see clearly the beauty in the lessons.

It is important to understand that the stories we carry have a plethora of lessons weaved within them. As we clear out the cobwebs of painful emotions, we can see clearly the beauty in the lessons.

I invite you to go through this exercise to help you discover what you are ready to let go of now.

Grab a pen and paper and write down your most intense stories, including things that were out of your control. They may be past failures you have not yet forgiven. They may include a car accident or your failing health. They might include forgiving something that happened in a relationship. Your list could include the passing of a loved one, a divorce, or a financial failure. For some, it could include regret over how you parented your children. It could be a vile, hurtful act that was committed against you. They could be situations you allowed to continue even though you knew you deserved better. Be sure to include things you think you may have overcome already. Be honest with yourself, and write down all the stories you are not yet free of.

Now we are going to focus on the emotions related to these stories. This method can be useful if you do not have access to a coach or healer who can guide you into deeper release. This simple step-by-step process can be done solo, but it does take practice. Don't get frustrated with it. Know that just going through the steps will begin releasing whatever you are holding on to a little bit at a time. The more you release, the more you begin to feel lighter, more joyful, and freer.

Scan your list of experiences and pinpoint what it is you feel you are ready to let go of. Find a comfortable spot with no one around. Close your eyes. Breathe deeply until you are in a fully relaxed state. Allow the memory to come up. Feel every part of this memory. Put yourself back in time. What are you experiencing with your senses? Follow the steps below to pinpoint and release the emotion:

Discover how you are experiencing this emotion. What does it feel like? Where are you experiencing it in your body?

Allow the emotion to sit with you. Close your eyes and fully experience it.

Get out of your head and put full emphasis on where you feel the emotion. Quiet any conversations going on in your head. Focus your full attention on the emotion.

You may find that the emotion begins to feel more intense. Allow it.

Ask yourself, "When was the first time I experienced this emotion?" Keep your eyes closed and allow yourself to return to that place and time. Fully allow and experience the emotion related to that experience. What is coming up for you right now using all five senses? Place yourself into the story as if you are watching a movie. Whichever details come up, allow the experience to unfold visually as if you were there in that space and time right now.

Next, ask yourself, "Am I willing to let this emotion go now?" Reply with, "Yes." Next state, "I am giving my unconscious mind permission to let go of this emotion that is no longer serving me."

Ask yourself, "If this emotion had a shape, what shape would it be? If this emotion had a color, what color would it be? Where is this emotion in my body right now?"

Visualize in whatever way comes naturally to you that this emotion is now leaving your body. When I do this with my older daughter, she visualizes giving it to God's outstretched hands.

Then ask yourself, "What are the positive messages I can take from this story?" Then ask, "How can I change my perception of this story?"

Then continue the process by asking yourself where else this emotion has shown up. Go through memory by memory. Let go of the emotion no longer serving you, take with you the positive messages, and change your perception of the story.

You may find that releasing the emotion comes in layers. It could come up again while you are making dinner, driving down the road, or watching your child playing and realizing you were their age when something painful happened. When this happens and you are not in a space where you can close your eyes and go into a deeper state of release, you can still ask yourself the series of questions and make the release statements to help dissipate it until you can do the deeper work.

When I first had these steps for anger release performed on me, the experience was more profound than attempting release techniques on myself. Four stories related to anger came up for me. I visualized and felt the anger leaving my body. The healing was intense, and immediately following the release, I entered into a beautiful, blissful, and joyful state. For more than a week afterwards, I felt a hole in my heart where I had previously stored this anger. It was like this toxic, emotional cyst had been feeding off of my heart, and then suddenly, it was surgically removed. My family noticed I was more joyful and smiling more. While I could still feel the scar for several days afterwards, my heart muscle was stronger and free from it. We had reprogrammed those stories in my unconscious mind, creating new neuropathways to a perception that better served me. I still find, since that release, I am not as easily triggered to anger, and when something does come up, I turn it around quickly.

Another release method is Emotional Freedom Technique (EFT). Originally created by Gary Craig, an ordained minister and NLP Practitioner, and reignited by Nick Ortner in the book *The Tapping Solution for Manifesting Your Greatest Self*, this technique was taught to orphaned genocide survivors in Rwanda to help heal their Post-Traumatic Stress Disorder (PTSD), and they paid it forward to the Sandy Hook survivors in Connecticut. *When I Was Young I Said I Would Be Happy* is a documentary showcasing Lori Leyden's work using EFT in Project LIGHT to bring awareness and release for the PTSD survivors of Rwanda and Sandy Hook. EFT is proven to be very effective for trauma and releasing painful emotions. When I tried EFT many years ago on myself, I found that the tapping and affirmations helped dissipate a lot of the painful emotions I was experiencing.

To release the emotion, you simply tap on specific meridian points on your body. Tap with either your index finger and middle finger together, or you can use four fingers. Use your fingertips, or if you have long nails, you can use your finger pads.

Say repeatedly as you are tapping on the points: "Even though I feel _____, I deeply and completely love and accept myself."

Use the following sequence in the tapping:

1. The karate chop part of the hand, located at the center of the fleshy part between the base of the pinky finger and the top of the wrist

2. Top of the head with fingers back-to-back down the center of the skull

3. Eyebrow just above and to one side of the nose, at the beginning of the eyebrow

4. Side of the eye

5. Under the eye

6. Under the nose

7. Chin

8. Collarbone

9. Under the arm

The redundancy makes this effective. It is important to allow yourself to feel the emotions. When you experience painful emotions, they are simply energy blocks in your system. With practice you can allow them, thank them, and release them. This exercise is also quite powerful while looking into your own eyes in the mirror. If you can do it in the mirror, also include the words, "I forgive you."

For example: "Even though _____, I love and accept myself and I forgive myself. I was doing the best I could."

> *Sometimes a big shift comes by just realizing that everyone is making the best choices they can given their own state of awareness. Some of the pain that continues to present itself to be healed just requires a shift in perspective.*

It is also powerful to tap while reciting your "I am" statements and affirmations aloud and looking into your own eyes in the mirror. This process is great for weight loss, public speaking, easing anxiety, and to attract love and success.

Many other modalities using specific language techniques speak directly into the unconscious and help reframe these experiences. Sometimes a big shift comes by just realizing that everyone is making the best choices they can given their own state of awareness. Some of the pain that continues to present itself to be healed just requires a shift in perspective.

You can ask yourself, "Is my perception of these stories serving my higher good?" If you feel you are weighed down by the emotions you are processing as if you are a prisoner to your own story, it is time to shift perspective. You cannot smell, taste, or touch these stories in the present moment, yet your yearning love, not fitting in, loneliness, anger, resentment, and sadness feel very real. Before I was aware that I could change my perspective of my story, all these similar emotions became a part of me, like clouds covering up the sunshine. Carrying around these emotions held me back from really connecting to people and allowing myself to be vulnerable. It was very rare that I would let anyone in and share my story. I lived my life in striving and accomplishing mode, and only a handful of people knew I struggled with connection.

> *You can ask yourself, "Is my perception of these stories serving my higher good?"*

As I became aware that my emotional attachments to these stories were what was holding me back from unleashing into my greatness, I began to take an inventory of my entire life, say yes to the healers who offered me these life-changing modalities, and completely change the perception of my childhood. This change in perception included a massive shift toward gratitude. I began writing down the parts of my story that pained me, and I asked myself, "Where have I taken on this story of pain, as the story of my life? Where have I chosen a disempowering perception of this experience rather than wrapping the experience in a reverence and acknowledging that I am in control of my thoughts, emotions, and the present moment?"

Take the list of experiences you wrote down earlier in this chapter. I invite you to change the script of these stories. What were the rich lessons in these stories? How did these stories make you stronger, more empowered, more willing to be guided, more empathetic, more compassionate, more loving, more peaceful, more intuitive, more creative, and more grateful? How can you take the disempowering emotions associated with these stories and replace them with compassion toward that person or experience and compassion toward yourself? What will it take to move the lever from one end of the spectrum—disempowerment—to the other end of the spectrum—reverence?

> ### What will it take to move the lever from one end of the spectrum–disempowerment–to the other end of the spectrum–reverence?

Journal your responses here:

_____

_____

_____

_____

_____

_____

_____

_____

Letting go is a powerful way to rise into your deeper purpose. The true rising occurs when you surrender, let go, embody compassion, and see that everything is all divinely orchestrated. Your life, previously perceived as imperfectly incomplete, is actually whole and perfect. Everything that tore you down actually caused you to rise up stronger. The strength is in the awareness and the vulnerability of letting go. When you allow yourself to be vulnerable, to let go of the emotions that do not serve you anymore, and change the perception of your stories, you will find that your true essence—the gifts of peace, unconditional love, and joy—are unleashed. In seeing the bigger picture of your story in this way, you will have more to celebrate in your life.

CHAPTER 9

The Power of Affirmations

*I am: Two of the most powerful words, for what
you put after them shapes your reality.*

— BEVAN LEE

Affirmations can be a powerful tool in reprogramming mindsets and unconscious beliefs that no longer serve you, as long as you are willing to heal what comes up. If you are moving further into the unleashing of your mission and truly begin to stretch yourself into something greater, anything that has not been fully healed from the first story of your life will show up.

I once was listening to Steven Aitchison, a self-improvement blogger and founder of Your Digital Formula, on Facebook Live. The topic was Seven Affirmations to Tell Yourself Daily. I stopped dead in my tracks when he mentioned the affirmation, "I am worthy." Immediately, I felt this overwhelming emotion of sadness and despair. I cried and felt that cry from the deepest parts of my soul. The incident that came up for me is a memory I cannot even consciously recall that happened when I was just four.

When reciting that affirmation aloud, it brought up the feeling of despair I experienced when my mother left. She was so distraught with grief and resentment over a failing marriage that she felt the best choice she could make at the time was to leave in the night while we slept, to soften her departure for all of us. Reciting the affirmation, I felt for the first time that her leaving had affected me. I have no conscious recollection of waking up the morning after she left and finding out that my mother was gone. I don't know if my father and siblings helped me process what happened or if it was another thing that was swept under the rug. I have no recollection of her being my mother at all, other than during the one or two weeks in the summers that I spent with her after the divorce.

The only memories I have are being raised by my father and step-mother. However, many years ago, I forgave my mother as best I could. I created a relationship with her in my adult life and empa-thized with her decision because of the difficult circumstances of the split. It really came as a surprise that this affirmation, "I am worthy," brought up such deep emotion from me related to this trauma. I realized that, while I may have fully forgiven her, I had not even come close to healing myself.

I had assumed that, since I had no memory of her being my mother or leaving, it had not affected me. What I didn't realize is that I had been storing my feelings of abandonment inside for thirty-plus years. Somehow, I had kept them tucked away safely in my uncon-scious mind so my conscious self would not have to deal with it.

More than thirty years later, there I sat in my ugly cry, reciting the affirmation, "I am worthy," over and over while more and more emotion bubbled up to the surface. I wondered whether anyone had ever helped me process what happened. I felt angry at myself for allowing this feeling of unworthiness to affect my entire life to its core. I thought of every failure and every time I felt inferior. I realized this feeling had affected all my relationships. I had built a wall around my emotions and didn't allow many people in. While I was charismatic and outgoing on the surface, few knew about my struggles. I didn't allow them in.

It was time to heal this once and for all.

I used muscle testing (applied kinesiology) to test the percentage of my alignment with the affirmation. It showed I was only 20 percent congruent with the "I am worthy" statement! After doing an emotional release practice that evening, it went up to 70 percent. By the next morning, I felt a bit lighter, and by the end of the week, I began to feel like a new person.

About nine months later, I was triggered again by this lingering feeling of unworthiness when a friend took advantage of my generosity, then disappeared out of my life. I again realized that healing traumatic emotions and forgiveness come in layers. I had attracted this situation to further heal my abandonment issues. I used the emotional release technique again to feel the feeling and gradually release the emotion. This brought my congruency up from 70 to 90 percent. The last time I checked, I was 99 percent congruent with the "I am worthy" statement, meaning that in my core I believe 99 percent that "I am worthy."

I am sure there is another layer there: the 1 percent. Jumping from 20 percent to 99 percent, can you imagine the difference? Working on the affirmation "I am worthy" opened up an entirely new path for me. I began to attract incredible experiences and kind-hearted, influential people. My life just kept getting better and better, and my heart opened more to trusting people and believing I could accomplish my dreams.

Affirmations can be a powerful tool in reprogramming mindsets and unconscious beliefs that no longer serve you, as long as you are willing to heal what comes up.

Why are these *I am* statements so powerful? Science shows that by regularly practicing self-affirmations, you can reduce the impact of stress and affect your willingness to make positive change in your life. I return again to one of the basic golden rules spoken by Jesus: "Love your neighbor as yourself." To love your neighbor, you must first love yourself. Practicing self-love in the physical world and re-programming our brains from running unconscious programming like: "I am not loved; I am not enough; I am not worthy," and replacing them with: "I am love; I am loved; I am enough; I am worthy," leads to our ability to have deeper compassion, love, and connection with ourselves, God, and, in turn, others.

The words we speak after "I am" are like a prayer. The words we speak after "I am" can determine what we attract. Any resistance to the affirmations helps us determine the darker parts of ourselves that keep us from our greatest potential. When we are willing to face and release attachment to our darkness, we begin to align our energy with astounding experiences and attract people who will comple-ment our vision. Everything and everyone will begin to show up for us, helping us fulfill our deeper mission.

When I work with my clients, if they experience blocks to crafting their story or rising out of their comfort zone in their business, we find the root cause of their perceived unworthiness, release the emotions, change the perception of their story, and layer in I am statements. I ask them to post their I am statements everywhere in their house, on their bathroom mirror, in the refrigerator, in their work area, on the inside of the front door so they see them before they head out for the day—anywhere they will be a constant reminder of their new reverent way of being.

> *When we are willing to face and release attachment to our darkness, we begin to align our energy with astounding experiences and attract people who will complement our vision.*

AN EXERCISE IN CREATING YOUR I AM STATEMENT:

Besides "I am worthy," "I am enough," and "I am loved," it can be fun creating more specific I am statements related to your core values, being, and dreams. It is important when creating your I am statement that you do it when you feel most connected, most alive, and positive. The best way to put yourself in this state is first to use the tools earlier in the book to unleash yourself from debilitating emotions and your disempowerment story. Then do what is necessary to practice self-love so you are in a state to receive. It may help to exercise first, pray, or meditate on your most joyful moment, and allow yourself to embody gratitude. Once you feel you are in your zone, look at the following "being" words, and pick the six that resonate most with you.

Abundant	Adventurous	Alive	Amazing	Assertive
Attentive	Audacious	Authentic	Awake	Awesome
Balanced	Beautiful	Blissful	Bold	Brave
Bright	Brilliant	Calm	Capable	Caring
Charismatic	Charming	Cherished	Clever	Committed
Compassionate	Complete	Confident	Connected	Conscious
Courageous	Creative	Daring	Delicious	Delightful
Dependable	Deserving	Determined	Devoted	Divine
Dynamic	Eager	Empathetic	Empowered	Empowering
Encouraging	Energetic	Enlightened	Entertaining	Enthusiastic
Exhilarated	Extraordinary	Exquisite	Fabulous	Fearless
Free	Fun	Generous	Genuine	Giving
Glorious	Graceful	Gracious	Grateful	Gregarious
Handsome	Happy	Harmonious	Healing	Healthy
Honorable	Honest	Humble	Innovative	Inspirational
Intelligent	Intuitive	Joyful	Kind	Limitless
Lovable	Loving	Loyal	Memorable	Mindful
Motivated	Nurturing	Outstanding	Open-minded	Optimistic
Passionate	Peaceful	Persuasive	Playful	Positive
Powerful	Prosperous	Radiant	Reliable	Remarkable
Resilient	Resourceful	Respectful	Reverent	Secure
Sensational	Sexy	Significant	Skillful	Smart
Sophisticated	Spectacular	Spiritual	Spontaneous	Stable
Strong	Successful	Supportive	Surrendered	Terrific
Transformational	Trustworthy	Trusting	Unapologetic	Unleashed
Unique	Unwavering	Valuable	Vibrant	Victorious
Visionary	Vivacious	Vulnerable	Whole	Wild
Willing	Winning	Wise	Wonderful	Worthy

BEING WORDS:

Being words:

_____ _____ _____ _____ _____ _____

Now choose three words below that best describe who you are or what you do that provides value.

Advisor	Artist	Author	Awakener	Being	Brother
CEO	Champion	Coach	Connector	Creator	Designer
Director	Doctor	Encourager	Enlightener	Entertainer	Entrepreneur
Father	Facilitator	Freelancer	Game Changer	Guide	Guru
Healer	Influencer	Instructor	Instrument of _	Leader	Lover
Man of God	Mentor	Mother	Peacemaker	Producer	Professor
Redeemer	Servant	Sister	Soul	Speaker	Spirit
Teacher	Visionary	Warrior	Woman of God	World Changer	Writer

VALUE WORDS:

Value words:

_____   _____   _____

Next, out of the six Being and three Value words, choose three to four Being words that best describe your optimal self—who you are rising up to *be*—and then add one or two Value words that best describes you. Fill in the blanks below for your I am statement:

I am a _____   _____   _____   _____

Now go to your bathroom mirror, and recite your I am statement until you really believe it. Don't just say it—shout it with all the enthusiasm you can muster. Shout it with gusto as you run around your home, tell your kids, tell your spouse, call your best friend, post it on your social media, scribble it on your mirror, post it on Post-it notes all over your house, and shout it to the rooftops. If you feel silly doing this, that's okay; just have fun with it! You have to feel it to your core. Continue reciting it boldly with intense vigor. Recite your I am statement every morning and evening and throughout the day.

When I first discovered my I am—"I am a reverent, loving, healing, bold leader and instrument of peace"—I had a couple of rough writing days where I wasn't feeling it. I went to my neighborhood coffee shop to write despite the writer's block I felt. I sat there and couldn't get my words out onto the page. I went into the bathroom and began jumping up and down shouting my I am statement until I felt it and shifted the block to gratitude. It worked! I realized I had allowed my inner critic to take over, and I wasn't allowing my true essence to come through. Reconnecting with my I am statement helped me dissolve the block.

You can create other *I am* statements related to your goals and the bigger vision for your life as well. For example, one of my affirmations is: "I feel happy and grateful that I am now impacting millions of lives with my Unleash Your Rising message." In creating that affirmation, I visualized what it would be like for people to find their voices and rise into deeper purposes in their lives. I visualized people like you feeling impacted by this book and sharing it with their friends and family. I closed my eyes and experienced feeling immensely grateful for being an instrument of change.

Below write three *I am* statements related to your vision and how you intend to rise to become a more impactful leader.

_____

_____

_____

When you create your *I am* statements, close your eyes and embody the vision. Allow yourself to feel the impact now. Stay connected with your *I am* statements throughout the day, every day. You will find you can accomplish more because you are pulled by a vision bigger than you.

CHAPTER 10

Understanding the Brain to Facilitate Life Change

Everything is first created in the mind.

— JOHN ASSARAF

CHANGING YOUR MINDSET AND BELIEF SYSTEMS

People live out their lives according to what they consciously and unconsciously think and believe about themselves and the world. Our thoughts and beliefs run on a conscious and unconscious level. Our beliefs are those we have taken on in our conscious minds based on our environment, what we were taught, and the sum of experiences we've had and judged. These are our religious and spiritual beliefs, beliefs about health, child-rearing, the vaccine schedule, the media, what happens when we die, what political party we follow, beliefs about money and our ability to attract it, beliefs about love, and even down to the car we drive and the cellphone brand we choose.

People live out their lives according to what they consciously and unconsciously think and believe about themselves and the world.

All these beliefs form first in our conscious brains; then our brain unconsciously finds evidence to support those beliefs. Our brains can only process 134 bits of information per second out of the two million bits of information coming into our sensory organs per second. Since the brain is constantly working to conserve energy, it will automatically grab on to any familiar information, and the rest it filters out, distorts, ignores, or generalizes. This is why changing your mindset and beliefs can be so difficult. If you are stuck in the feeling of lack because striving to achieve has resulted in lack, then that is all the brain will pick up on, and naturally, that is what will continue to manifest.

When you make the conscious choice to live in abundance, changing your mindset and beliefs around what it means to live in abundance, your brain will begin to find information that aligns with an abundance mindset. As you open your mind to a different set of thoughts and beliefs, your brain creates new neuropathways to accommodate the new beliefs. Then, as evidence or stimuli reinforces the new belief, the brain files it with the new beliefs and continues to find data that aligns with these new beliefs.

A POWERFUL EXERCISE FOR BELIEFS:

One powerful way to break through limiting beliefs and replace them with new ones is by using this series of questions, in this order:

What belief is holding me back? Or, what is getting in my way?

Why do I believe that?

What am I fearful of?

What would happen if I stopped believing that?

Do I truly believe that?

Whose belief is it, really?

What can I choose to believe instead that would serve me in a positive way?

Notice how you feel the shift immediately when you question the limiting belief. As you make the choice to take on a more positive mindset, your brain will find data to align with the positive mindset and more positivity will manifest itself. The same is true for our perception of the world as a whole. As Wayne Dyer said, "Loving people live in a loving world. Hostile people live in a hostile world. Same world."

As you open your mind to a different set of thoughts and beliefs, your brain creates new neuropathways to accommodate the new beliefs. Then, as evidence or stimuli reinforces the new belief, the brain files it with the new beliefs and continues to find data that aligns with these new beliefs.

Essentially, our reality is a combination of our thoughts, beliefs, and mindset, all originating in the mind. We can retrain our minds and, in turn, change our reality. This brain alignment is the same for goal-setting. As you create goals, especially if you are documenting them, visualizing them in more relaxed, yet higher amplitude brain wave states, and reviewing them consistently, your brain will notice data and opportunities that align with your goals to help make them a reality. Your brain will always look for what is familiar, and that becomes your reality.

Now that we understand the brain can work for us if we choose to open up to new beliefs and make a conscious effort to change our mind and perceptions about our lives, we can go a step further and begin to use our brain to our advantage in healing parts of our lives that keep us stuck.

HEALING THE STUCK PARTS OF YOUR LIFE

Using visualization in the higher amplitude brain waves, in the unconscious, you can create new movies in your mind that align with a more joyful life. You can reframe memories, change your perception of past experiences, and visualize the future to facilitate positive life change. Rather than having your brain's default safety mechanisms hold you back, you can become the producer and director of your life's story. This means you can cut and move on to take two, take three, take four, take however many takes necessary to rise above the disempowering parts of your story and recreate your life.

Using visualization in the higher amplitude brain waves, in the unconscious, you can create new movies in your mind that align with a more joyful life. You can reframe memories, change your perception of past experiences, and visualize the future to facilitate positive life change. Rather than having your brain's default safety mechanisms hold you back, you can become the producer and director of your life's story.

Before diving into how this is possible, it is important to understand the five different brain wave states: beta, alpha, theta, delta, and gamma. Each frequency is measured in cycles per second (Hz). These brain waves can be measured using an electroencephalogram (EEG) machine. These varying frequencies can continuously shift from state to state throughout the day during normal brain processing in adults, and we can have more than one brain wave state operating at the same time at varying degrees.

Children, however, grow into different frequencies as they develop and age. The higher amplitude, slower brain wave frequencies of infants (delta) are more impressionable than the faster, more analytical brain wave frequencies they eventually grow into (beta). Delta (.1-3Hz) is the state adults enter into in deep sleep. Children move into theta around age two and remain there until somewhere between ages eight and twelve when beta brain waves begin to be introduced.

To facilitate life change, it is imperative to reformat our hard drive, so to speak. The only way to do so is to bring your brain back into the more impressionable states and download new information.

A child's first seven years are called the "imprint period," essentially because every bit of data is soaked up and imprinted. No filter regulates what goes in. All the data encountered during the first seven years of life is stored in the unconscious. The brain is wired at a very young age, and programs run in the background, the unconscious, while we consciously live our lives and respond to new experiences and new data. To facilitate life change, it is imperative to reformat our hard drive, so to speak. The only way to do so is to bring your brain back into the more impressionable states and download new information.

Beta—Your Logical, Analytical Mind

Beta brain wave state is our normal waking consciousness state. It has a frequency of fourteen to forty cycles per second (14-40Hz). This state is the seat of critical, logical, and analytical thinking and is reached between the ages of eight and twelve. This state is crucial to operating effectively throughout the day; however, it is also the state where negative thoughts can take over.

The voice of beta is often described as that nagging inner critic that can intensify the higher it goes in range. Beta puts people in a constant thinking and doing state, which can lead to anxiety and stress. I noticed when my seven-year-old began to enter into beta. She started analyzing scenarios, drawing her own conclusions, and asking more questions. I could tell when she was all wrapped up in her thoughts and in a state of constant doing. Sometimes it was evening before I could wind her back down into more relaxed brain wave states where more heartfelt connection takes place. I came to appreciate these quiet moments all the more, along with her charter school's practicing of mindfulness twice per day. Essentially, in doing so, children are taking a break from the logical, analytical parts of their brains and calming their nervous systems. As adults, it is also imperative to step out of the doing and thinking of beta to reconnect to a state of peace and calm.

Alpha—Reprogramming Trauma and Embodying Forgiveness

The alpha brain wave state is higher amplitude and runs at the slower rate of seven-and-a-half to fourteen cycles per second (7.5-

14Hz). This is the brain wave state people go into when they watch television. Advertisements and media coverage on television have such a strong influence because we are receiving the information at the entrance of our unconscious mind. Children between ages five and eight have a foot in both alpha and beta.

Alpha state is optimal for imagination, learning, brainstorming, and concentration. As adults, we can reach these states, typically by winding down by reading a book, doing aerobic exercise, relaxing in the bathtub, taking a shower, or closing our eyes to daydream mindfully or do a light meditation. This state serves as a gateway to your unconscious mind and lies at the base of your conscious awareness.

The most tuned-in intuition is received in the alpha brain wave states closer to 7.5Hz. Practicing, at minimum, light meditation or relaxed daydreaming can help program your mind for success. Here is where you can begin to harness your mind's creative power.

The higher amplitude alpha states are also powerful in healing trauma. Using visualization, you can cut the emotional cord to memories and wrap the story in light, love, and forgiveness. In alpha, you can visualize scenarios from your past and speak into the experience everything you deserve to say, essentially reprogramming your perception of the experience. From a scientific standpoint, you can create new neuropathways to any memory using lower alpha so you are no longer emotionally triggered by the memory.

When you are able to reach this level in healing, the next step is seeing the bigger picture of the experience, honoring your journey, honoring others' journeys, and shifting into gratitude for it all. When I was healing from the shame of being molested as a young child, it took layers of healing and layers of forgiveness. I first forgave my offender, but I realized I still harbored pain against the person who began the chain of abuse. Since there was a chain, it made it easier for me to forgive my offender because I knew this person had been acting upon what had happened to them.

Before I got pregnant with Grace, I became sensitive to the trauma these acts imposed upon other people in my family. I could feel the pain they were experiencing. I visited a healer, and in a session, she brought me into a deeply relaxed alpha brain wave state. I was able to confront the experience and say all I truly deserved to say to take a stand for my family. In doing so, I created a new neuropathway for that memory and was able to peel away these deeper layers of trauma and further forgive the experience.

Just one week after that healing session, I ended up attracting an encounter with the original offender who started this traumatic chain of sexual abuse in my family before I was even born. I had actually never met this person before, and the way our paths crossed that day was no coincidence since I had been setting an intention for the healing of all my family, not just me. Although I had never met this man, I was attached to the story of who he was and the pain he had caused other members of my family. While I forgave my offender—I still carried bitter resentment toward this person. Here I was presented with the opportunity to confront him in the flesh and tell him how his actions deeply affected our family. I was shaking in fear at the thought of confronting him, yet everything in me demanded that I do so, so I did.

Although he got angry and denied it, I was relieved that I had stood in my truth. Confronting him created the space for a conversation between a few other family members, stimulating healing and forgiveness.

A few years later, I had another opportunity to go into an alpha brain wave state to heal the final layers of this experience. I realized, after watching the documentary *The Power of the Heart*, that while I had confronted this person and helped facilitate further healing for my family, it had not occurred to me back then to forgive him. He was not remorseful, so that probably didn't help. I realized that at some point, I was going to have to see this person again, likely at the next family funeral, so I closed my eyes and put myself in a deeply relaxed state, as if I were drifting off to sleep. In this state, I saw a movie unfold in my mind of the funeral. As the story unfolded, I saw this person across the table as we were getting food. We both looked up, and our eyes met. It was him. I immediately felt a release of all resentment toward him. I looked him directly in the eyes, and said, "I forgive you." Then I felt a rush of love flow through me, and I found myself saying, "You are forgiven."

The second message did not come from me; it came *through* me, as God speaking through me. In hearing it, I felt a huge shift. My heart filled up with gratitude, and using visualization, I wrapped him and all the experiences associated with him in a tornado of the bright, white light of forgiveness. I cut the disempowering emotional cord to all those experiences. I was no longer attached to the story of what had happened; I shifted to an honoring of his journey. I then set the intention that he would feel an energy shift and feel forgiven as well. That day, I was set free from the trauma by creating a new neuropathway to that memory, and from a spiritual perspective, I embodied unconditional love, which heals and forgives all.

Using similar visualization techniques in alpha can reprogram your mind for success and help you manifest more love and abundance.

Theta—Making the Shift from Unworthiness to Reverence

Feelings of unworthiness can originate as early as in the womb. Just as we can feel the energy if someone is emotionally invested in us, an unborn children can pick up on whether or not they are wanted. As newborns take in all the sights, sounds, and responses from their environment, they are also drawing conclusions in their unconscious minds, calculating their worthiness based on how people respond to their basic needs for love, interaction, food, and care. This imprint period from the womb all the way up to approximately seven years old is critical since the child's theta brain wave state is the same brain wave state used to bring people into hypnosis.

The theta state, found in two- to six-year-olds, runs at a frequency of four to seven-and-a-half cycles per second (4-7.5Hz). Theta is the state entered into during deep meditation. Essentially, children in this age range are exploring and receiving information all day in a hypnotic state. This critical period is building an unconscious platform for how children view themselves and their environment.

In theta, the unconscious state, we are better able to see the big picture of our lives and receive heightened insight. In the forgiveness visualization above, I can't be certain what state I was in, alpha or theta. We actually have all brain wave states working at the same time, yet with practice, we can shift which is dominant at any given time. I was likely in the alpha-theta border from 7Hz to 8Hz, where visualization and creative power are optimal in reprogramming the mind. In the deep, relaxed state of the alpha-theta border, you can create your own reality, yet you are still conscious of your surroundings. This is the gateway to intuition, where inspiration and profound reverence are ignited.

> *In the deep, relaxed state of the alpha-theta border, you can create your own reality, yet you are still conscious of your surroundings. This is the gateway to intuition, where inspiration and profound reverence are ignited.*

Do you remember your first memories as a child, when you were solely in the theta brain wave state? What are your first memories between the ages of two and seven? Look back and ask yourself what messages you received that programmed your self-worth and ability to give and receive love. As you began to dive into the power of your brain, you can instantly reprogram unconscious beliefs you inherited through painful experiences. Reprogramming your sense of self-worth can influence every aspect of your life in a powerful way. When you feel worthy and loved on a conscious and unconscious level, your thoughts, beliefs, and mindset will begin to show you what is possible. You are whole and complete. You can make a difference not by attempting to fix anything or anyone, but rather by focusing on changing yourself, which will create a ripple of transformation.

Gamma—Being in the Zone

Gamma is the next level of brain wave states. It measures between 25Hz and 100Hz, 40Hz being typical for most humans. Gamma brain waves are the fastest brain wave frequency, yet have the smallest amplitude.

These waves begin in the thalamus, moving from the back of the brain to the front and back again around forty times per second. Neuroscientists report that gamma waves link together all parts of the brain, increase gray matter, and improve neuroplasticity, or the brain's ability to form new neural connections. Gamma waves are associated with peak mental and physical performance, advanced memory recall, increased five-sensory perception, and increased focus. Feelings associated with this state include being in the zone, feeling you can do anything, and feeling blessed, happy, peaceful, and calm. High achievers, top musicians, and high-performance athletes all tend to have more gamma waves than the average person. On the flip side, people with learning disabilities, impaired mental function, depression, or memory issues have less gamma wave activity.

Gamma waves are associated with peak mental and physical performance, advanced memory recall, increased five-sensory perception, and increased focus. Studies show that meditation with a focus on compassion and love can help increase gamma wave activity.

You may ask, "How can I increase gamma wave activity?" Studies show that meditation with a focus on compassion and love can help increase gamma wave activity. These studies reveal an increase of activity in the left, prefrontal cortex (associated with self-control, empathy, happiness, and compassion) and decreased activity in the amygdala, the fight-or-flight part of the brain. Brain scans of Celestine nuns and Tibetan monks who regularly practice love and compassion-meditation show that, overall, activity in the amygdala decreases and their left, prefrontal cortex is highly active.

Loving-kindness meditation is another type of meditation that stimulates the prefrontal cortex. It does so by focusing on developing feelings of goodwill, kindness, positive wellbeing, and warmth toward others. Eighteen separate studies reveal that loving-kindness meditation activates empathy and compassion, increases emotional intelligence, reduces stress responses, reduces PTSD, decreases migraines, helps heal physical and mental ailments, increases feelings of social connection, increases helping behavior, improves self-compassion, helps with emotional regulation, decreases schizophrenia-spectrum disorders, decreases chronic pain and anger, increases overall positive emotions, and even decreases biological markers of aging.

Overall, by reducing the overactive, thinking parts of your brain and layering in compassion-focused intention, you are able to better connect to the power of the heart, receive answers to the deeper questions of life, and lead your life with ultimate intuition and pure creativity. You can achieve these awake states all day long, just by having a regular exercise routine and practicing mindfulness and reverent intention throughout the day. You will find it easier to stay focused in the present moment, and you will be fueled with energy. The disempowerment states of first story will remain at bay while your true essence of third story, compassion, gratitude, peace, love, and joy shines through. This is how you can attract the love of your life, meaningful friendships, and become a more impactful leader of yourself and others.

Understand that the brain can facilitate not only life change, but also world change. The reverent intention you put out into the world can create a massive shift as you develop a higher sense of oneness with all of humanity.

REVERENCE MEDITATION EXERCISE:

Find a comfortable position in a chair with your legs uncrossed, feet flat on the floor, hands palms up, lying comfortably on your legs or off to the side. Close your eyes and just relax your body. Bring your awareness inward. Take a deep breath in and breathe out. Take another deep breath in and breathe out until you feel completely calm and relaxed. Visualize a person who loves you very much. This could be a family member, alive or deceased, a spiritual teacher, or your creator. Imagine the person is sending you all the love they have for you. They are sending you intentions of safety and infusing you with good health, peace, wellbeing, and joy. Fully embody all the warm feelings coming from this person. Now imagine another being in your life doing the same—and another and another, until you have all your friends and loved ones, past and present, surrounding you and sending you the intention of love, peace, good health, wellbeing, and joy. Allow yourself to be completely filled with these loving, kind, reverent feelings. You are overflowing with warmth and love.

Now send all of these loving, kind, reverent intentions back to your friends and loved ones one by one, infusing them with love, peace, safety, good health, and joy. Just like you, your friends and loved ones wish for happiness, joy, and good health. Recite in your mind three times, silently: *Just as I wish, may you too be loved. May you feel safe. May you live with ease and good health. I fill myself up with compassion for you and I send you love, joy, and peace.*

Then extend it out to people whom you may see in passing, people whom you do not know well, including neighbors, colleagues, the person ringing up your groceries, children playing on a nearby playground, and people in leadership. Recite in your mind three times, silently: *Just as I wish, may you too be loved. May you feel safe. May you live with ease and good health. I fill myself up with compassion for you and I send you love, joy, and peace.*

Now extend the loving-kindness intentions out to those who are unfortunate or suffering. Recite in your mind three times, silently: *Just as I wish, may you too be loved. May you feel safe. May you live with ease and good health. I fill myself up with compassion for you and I send you love, joy, and peace.*

Now extend this loving-kindness out to everyone on the planet, infusing all of humanity with loving, kind, reverent intentions. Recite in your mind three times, silently: *Just as I wish, may you too be loved. May you feel safe. May you live with ease and good health. I fill myself up with compassion for you and I send you love, joy, and peace.*

Truly take in what it feels like to be an instrument of reverence, embodying compassion, gratitude, peace, love, joy, and good health.

Take a deep breath in and breathe out. Take another deep breath in and breathe out—breathing in reverence, breathing out reverence. When you are ready, you may open your eyes.

Understand that the brain can facilitate not only life change, but also world change. The reverent intention you put out into the world can create a massive shift as you develop a higher sense of oneness with all of humanity.

CHAPTER 11

Living a Healthy Life

No person may enjoy outstanding success without good health.

— NAPOLEON HILL

In order to unleash your highest potential, it is important to be in integrity with what your body requires. Your body is the instrument for all of your creative inspiration, your mindset, and your quality of life. I consider caring for your body a spiritual act. You are entrusted with this gift. When you care for your physical body, your spiritual being inside can vibrate at the highest possible frequency. I know when I am at my best in my health, I feel the most connected, more creative, and in a better space to serve others. When we slack off (and we all do!), either for a week or several years, the bottom line is we don't feel good about ourselves because we are out of integrity. Typically, when we aren't eating well and feel stressed out, other areas of our life are also out of integrity. The basis of most health issues today is a combination of poor diet, mineral/vitamin deficiencies, lack of exercise, subluxations in the body, and emotions or stress.

Your body is the instrument for all of your creative inspiration, your mindset, and your quality of life.

HOLISTIC HEALTH

Many of the changes to my health I can credit to my chiropractor, Dr. Chris Hengesteg. He implements a combination of chiropractic, whole-food nutraceuticals, and emotional release in his practice. When we first met through friends in 2005, he encouraged me to come in to see him for my lower back pain related to a bulging torn disk. I had accepted the fact that I would live with the pain the rest of my life after trying the conventional approach. Despite my hesitancy to step foot into a chiropractor's office, he convinced me he could not only help my lower back, but he had other tools to help me get my health on track. During my first visit, he began using muscle testing, also called applied kinesiology, to determine the best way to adjust my lower back. After the adjustments I felt relief from the pain right away. I was stunned when, two hours later, my menstrual cycle started. This may not appear to be a big deal, but I had not had my cycle for more than six months. Then I had an aha moment. The lower back adjustment helped stimulate the nerves connected to my reproductive organs. In that moment, and as I achieved 100 percent recovery, I became a believer in the power of chiropractic.

In subsequent visits, Dr. Chris began testing me and found that I had a buildup of candida and bacteria in my body. The candida buildup likely explains my sugar cravings and loss of energy over the prior year. The dormant bacteria clearly explains why I got bronchitis every year. He used the same muscle testing to find which supplements my body responded positively to. When I questioned how my arm could go weak on some supplements and strong on others, he replied simply, "It's quantum physics." He performed a test where I put my arm out and he asked me to state: "My name is Christine." While I said it, he applied firm pressure on my arm to push it down and my arm remained strong. He then asked me to say, "My name is Mary." To my astonishment, at that false statement, my arm went weak no matter how hard I tried keeping it up while he applied the same firm pressure. This was the first time after studying Freud in college that I personally understood and realized the power of my unconscious mind. My conscious mind had no power over my body when I stated a falsehood. I was amazed how my unconscious mind, where my true name was engrained since birth, had more control over my conscious mind.

I began to wonder what else my unconscious mind had control over. It wasn't until I began studying neuroscience, the power of affirmations, and how each part of the brain functions that all of this came together. All I knew back then was that the supplements I tested strong for made my body feel healthier. I learned that rather than taking oral antibiotics that wiped out the good bacteria in my gut when I was fighting a virus, I could take a supplement with bovine thymus gland in it or larch tree extract, get a chiropractic adjustment, do some emotional release, and feel fine within a few days. For the first time in years, I did not get bronchitis! I became more attuned to my body and what I put into it. If I went on a sugar and carb binge, the candida would sneak back. I would feel bloated, tired, foggy-headed, moody, and sluggish. With probiotics and another supplement containing undecylenic acid and olive leaf extract, I would feel like myself again. I began to realize I could only sustain eating carbs and sugar in small amounts.

I began testing all of my shampoos, detergents, and cleaning solutions in my home and discovered that products I had been using for years made my body weak. It became clear that chiropractic using applied kinesiology was the saving grace for my living pain-free and what I put into and onto my body truly mattered.

EMOTIONAL HEALTH

As the months went by, I visited my chiropractor regularly for checkups. I began to discover that when I experienced stress, my lower back would start hurting again. He used muscle testing to determine what specific emotions were related to my back pain. He went a step further to test when I first experienced the emotion in my life, and then he would walk me through simple steps to release it. Deep-rooted traumas I had no idea were affecting me came up in these sessions. It was mind-boggling to me that I could come in with lower back pain and it would go away by using this simple emotional release technique, even without a chiropractic adjustment. As I grew to trust him more, I was amazed that we could find other emotions stored in various parts of the body. For example, grief is stored in the lung point. He shared with me the first time he had been introduced to the notion that emotions affected his body. Like me, he at first did not understand the correlation between emotion and the body and laughed it off. At a conference, however, it hit him hard that he was holding on to deep-seated grief related to watching his mother fight cancer for six-and-a-half years, then pass away at the young age of fifty. This was his first introduction to the power of emotional release therapy and the stepping stone for his full recovery from gastrointestinal issues, fatigue, and food sensitivities. I found that the more I released, the more freedom I felt. Emotional release is a powerful tool you can use to stimulate healing in your body. Letting go of emotions that do not serve you can also stimulate spiritual growth.

NOURISHING FOOD

So what about food? The way my seven-year-old describes the body makes perfect sense: "Your body is nature." If your body is nature, doesn't it make sense to feed it what comes from nature? All the elements from the earth are meant to nourish our bodies. The closer to the source of life, the better. Food that comes in a box or a package is the furthest from life. The human body typically maintains a pH of just above seven, and it will fight to maintain this alkaline state. When we feed our body low alkaline foods, it will borrow the small amount of minerals in our body to compensate. Creating this internal battle creates migraines, fatigue, premature aging, a low sex drive, brain fog, and disconnection from creative flow.

Eating foods that reduce inflammation can decrease the likelihood of inflammation-based diseases like rheumatoid arthritis, fibromyalgia, or heart disease. Diet plays a key role in maintaining healthy cell life for healthy aging, a clear mind, and overall feeling good. It is our goal in eating more alkaline, antioxidant, and inflammation-reducing foods to give our body what it needs to function at its highest state of health. Begin feeding your body higher-alkaline, "life food" that reduces inflammation and oxidative stress. When you can, choose organic over conventional. Eat less meats and more vegetables. When you are craving dessert, eat fruit. Eat as much raw food as you can. Eat smaller meals more often, and incorporate green smoothies. The side effects? Weight loss, improved energy and focus, clarity and concentration, a healthy emotional life, better sleep, an improved immune system, healthier skin, and healthier aging.

The key is to start small and work your way into healthier eating. Which of the following foods can you begin incorporating into your diet? Spinach, kale, broccoli, green beans, red beets, grapefruit, mangoes, blueberries, avocados, melons, lemons, limes, cucumbers, carrots, cabbage, celery, apples, citrus, pineapple, figs, dates, almonds, pumpkin seeds, sunflower seeds, green tea, water from a spring, mineral water, unsweetened almond milk, coconut water, wheat grass, alfalfa grass, oregano, parsley, ginger, sprouts, Himalayan salt, small amounts of gluten-free/yeast-free sprouted breads, walnuts, black grapes, goji berries, elderberries, cacao nibs, and turmeric.

Brain Nutrients

The brain is made up of approximately 60 percent fat, so it is imperative to consume healthy fats like: avocados, avocado oil, eggs with the yolk, wild fish, coconut oil, coconut cream, flax oil, sesame oil, almonds, almond butter, clarified (ghee) butter, and butter from grass-fed sources. Other components that elevate brain health are Omega-3s with DHA and EPA, choline, magnesium l-threonate, turmeric, coffee berry, ashwagandha, lion's mane, vinpocetine, phosphatidylserine, acetyl-L-carnitine, ginkgo biloba, phosphatidylcholine, SAM-e, CoQ10, and B vitamins.

SUGAR AND YOUR HEALTH

Sugar and foods/drinks that turn to sugar in the body are a major dietary issue. The United States has the highest sugar consumption per capita in the world. The average American consumes three pounds of sugar a week! Most people do not realize how much they are consuming until they begin reading ingredients: cane sugar, evaporated cane syrup, brown sugar, brown rice syrup, barley malt, corn syrup, coconut palm sugar, dextrose, fructose, lactose, maltose, and glucose are all sugars hidden in foods, causing all types of health issues. Studies show that sugar inhibits the brain-derived neurotrophic factors (BDNF) responsible for learning and creating new memories. When our BDNF is low, our memory is affected. Links have been made between low BDNF and depression, Alzheimer's, and dementia. Another form of sugar is alcohol. Alcohol turns to sugar in the body and is a depressant. It is common for alcoholics to turn to sugar when they are in remission. Studies have shown that sugar feeds cancer cells, lowers the immune system, and has the same addictive effect on the brain as cocaine.

Sugar and Consciousness

When I began taking sugar out of my diet for long stretches starting in 2005, I noticed a huge difference in my ability to feel spiritually connected and get into the creative flow. More recently, I noticed being sugar free also improves my ability to be in the moment and respond with more patience and love with my children. Anytime I begin to consistently partake in sugar again, then attempt to wean off of it, I feel like an addict and suffer withdrawal symptoms like moodiness, cravings, and headaches. As I became more aware of my body and moods, I saw a high correlation between sugar and my overall emotional and spiritual health. When I began the process of writing this book, I took reducing my sugar intake more seriously to keep my mind clear for the inspiration to flow.

If you would like to experiment, try taking sugar out of your diet during the week, and then treat yourself to one treat over the weekend. Eventually, when the weekend comes and it is time to have the treat, ask yourself, "What is truly the root of this craving? Do I really want this? Will this serve my higher self? How have I been feeling without it?" You may find that you feel better bypassing it altogether. I have now reduced my consumption to just a few bites on special occasions. That way, I am still partaking when we are celebrating, but I am not compromising my health. Weaning yourself off sugar can feel effortless after you get past the first week. Eat smaller healthier meals more often, ensure you are getting enough magnesium, exercise regularly, and be generous with cinnamon in your green shakes to minimize insulin spikes.

Sugar Cravings

For stress-induced sugar cravings, go for a walk, do jumping jacks, organize your closet, or call a friend. Go within and ask yourself, "Why am I having this craving? What is really going on that I am looking to mask it with sugar?" One way to bypass the cravings is to eat a piece of fruit, stevia-sweetened dark chocolate, or drink a stevia or monk fruit-sweetened chocolate protein shake with unsweetened almond milk. If you have time to bake, try the paleo, no-sugar recipes online that use natural sweeteners like dates, honey, applesauce, monk fruit, and organic stevia. Typically, once you are off sugar for thirty days, unless you are experiencing stress, when someone offers you a sugar-filled treat, you will be able to pass it up and go for the fruit or veggie tray with no cravings or feelings of missing out.

EXERCISE AND METABOLISM

When it comes to exercise, the key is to stay consistent. You don't have to do long, aerobic workouts every day. Instead, focus on getting twenty to thirty minutes of aerobic activity three to five times per week and include weight training to tone your muscles. With leaner muscle mass, you will automatically burn more calories. Exercise will naturally boost your metabolism, enhance your brain health, and reduce depression and anxiety.

PLAN OUT A WEEKLY EXERCISE REGIME:

Monday: _____

Tuesday: _____

Wednesday: _____

Thursday: _____

Friday: _____

Saturday: _____

Sunday: _____

THE POWER OF SLEEP

I found when I was deep in writing this book, I could live with less sleep as long as I got a twenty-minute nap later in the day. Also, when I experienced fatigue from staring at the computer screen for too long, I would drift off with the help of a guided sleep meditation on my phone and set my alarm for twenty minutes, waking up fully refreshed and ready to write some more. This inspired me to research what happens in the brain when we nap.

Despite the fact that 40 percent of Americans get less than six hours of sleep per night, our body requires seven to eight hours of sleep. But if you are powering through a project, like writing a book or creating a new program at work, try power napping. Research shows that a twenty-minute nap can increase cognitive function by 40 percent, and our brain has the most clarity after a restful nap.

Our memory also improves if we nap. Participants in a study memorized illustrated cards, then took a forty-minute break. One group napped on the break and the other stayed awake. After the break, both groups were tested on their memory of the cards. The nappers remembered 85 percent of the cards, compared to the non-nappers who remembered 60 percent. When we wake from a nap, we are refreshed and able to retain more information.

WATER

Remember that our bodies are made up of 50-65 percent water, depending on your body mass index. Your brain and heart are composed of 73 percent water. Your lungs are made up of a whopping 80 percent water. Each of our body's systems depends on water. Water flushes out toxins and carries necessary nutrients to our cells. Our bodies function better if we drink half our body weight in ounces every day. This may seem difficult. To make it more manageable, buy BPA-free water bottles and fill them up with spring water or mineral water the night before. You can diffuse lemon, lime, berries, cucumber, or superfood powders into the water. Drink water first thing in the morning, between every meal throughout the day, and before bed. I find when I drink more water, it curbs my appetite, improves my skin, and improves brain clarity.

DOING OR BEING

We live in a society where we are mostly in a doing mode. The to-do list can seem never-ending at times, and we can be consumed with doing. If you are consumed with doing, it can cause stress and activate the fight-or-flight response. To reset ourselves from the fight-or-flight state, we need to help our bodies relax and stay calm. I have found chiropractic, acupuncture, and massage to be great ways to help my body relax. Other helpful techniques are yoga, walking, meditation, mindfulness, and prayer. It takes practice, but it is possible to get through your to-do list in a calm, relaxed flow in your being state. The key is practicing present moment awareness, being aware of your thoughts and being aware of your breath. Another way is to go about your day connecting spiritually, staying grounded, and releasing attachments to the things you are doing. Recognize your way of being and how you are showing up in everything you do.

Realizing that you are a spiritual being having a physical experience will help keep you detached and in a responsive state, rather than a reactive state. Then you can respond in the higher calibrated levels of reverence. Keeping the body in this state serves as a foundation for your health.

GRATITUDE

Shifting all negative thoughts to gratitude will help you feel better overall.

To do this, sometimes it helps to write down ten things you are grateful for. When you focus on all you are grateful for, you will notice yourself feeling better right away. Focus on the goodness in people and you will notice your judgment and comparisons go away. Focus on the lesson in your experience and wrap it in gratitude. If someone triggers you, shift to gratitude and believe the person showed up for you as a teacher, bringing to light where you are hurting, where your judgments that cause separation lie, and where it will serve you to forgive and let go.

When I saw Tony Robbins speak in Los Angeles, the most inspiring thing he said was to turn expectation into appreciation. As you give up how things should be and embrace what is, you will feel more at peace.

Feeling gratitude is turning what you have into enough. It takes away the striving and the yearning. Shifting your vibrational frequency to gratitude helps shift fear-based thinking to love.

GRATITUDE EXERCISE:

Ten things I am most grateful for:

1. _____

2. _____

3. _____

4. _____

5. _____

6. _____

7. _____

8. _____

9. _____

10. _____

Think of your health like a scale. If you put elements into your body that tip the scale toward disease, you must balance that out through detoxing, healthy eating, exercise, and cultivating healthy emotional health; otherwise, you are creating the type of environment where disease can thrive. Research by Dr. Bruce Lipton, as recorded in his book *Biology of Belief*, questions the notion that cancer is genetic. His research points toward the validity of environmental influence over genetic makeup. The environment you create for your body can either cause a family history of cancer to be activated or it can promote the endurance of healthy cell life and overall disease-free aging.

For the next month when you are making choices about what you put into your body, I invite you to ask yourself: "Will this serve my higher good? If not, what is available to me that will nourish and strengthen my body?"

"Will this serve my higher good? If not, what is available to me that will nourish and strengthen my body?"

Choose food that is as close to the source of life as possible. Ask yourself, "How can I become more mindful of my health choices and really listen to what my body requires?"

ACTIVATING YOUR INNER CHILD

One of the best ways to remain young and healthy is to act young and healthy. Remember what it was like to be a child? When was the last time you skipped along on the street, played hopscotch, jumped on a trampoline, played tag, played music and danced in your living room, rode a bike, sang your favorite songs, dressed up in costume, or just approached your day from the eyes of your inner child? Imagine if you lived every moment with childlike magic and wonder. How much more joyful would your life be?

Imagine if you lived every moment with childlike magic and wonder.

INNER CHILD EXERCISE:

What could you do in the mornings, after work, and on the weekends to activate your inner child?

Ideas to activate my inner child:

_____

_____

_____

_____

_____

Your health and mission are directly related to one another. When you feel good, you feel more motivated to rise into something greater. Being reverent toward your body, you will have closer access to the still, quiet voice that guides you in your creative expression. By setting yourself free of emotional toxins, creating a more balanced, mindful state in your everyday life, on top of infusing loving intention into everything you put into your body, you can become more in harmony with spirit. As you honor your body, your temple, and make your health top priority, other parts of your life will naturally become activated.

Your health and mission are directly related to one another. When you feel good, you feel more motivated to rise into something greater.

CHAPTER 12

A Self-Leadership Roadmap

What you want to ignite in others, must first burn inside yourself.

— AURELIUS AUGUSTINUS

Being an effective leader does not begin with how you lead others, but rather it begins with how you effectively lead yourself. How you lead others is an extension of how you lead yourself. The two go hand in hand. A good question to ask yourself is, "Would I follow myself?" Where you are in *Your Story of Intention* will greatly influence how you lead yourself and others. If you are experiencing disempowering emotions and not allowing yourself to process and release them, you will likely be stuck in a thought-process loop that does not serve you.

The thing is, when you are in these states, typically you will not be conscious of it. If you are unaware of it, the default is to allow negative thoughts and past failures to govern your choices. The way our brains are made, as a safety mechanism, we document the pain and can remember painful experiences better than positive ones. It is easy to allow this part of our brains to take over unconsciously, and then we can become stuck.

A good question to ask yourself is, "Would I follow myself?"

You will find in this state that it is easy to judge others' beliefs and become offended easily. As you become more aware and practice monitoring your thoughts and emotions, you can move out of the lower disempowerment stages into the higher disempowerment stages. When this occurs, you may begin to get glimpses of the unleashing. For example, a peacefulness may come over you at times. You may even experience feelings of euphoria or bliss. This, at times, will wake you up, but until you do the deep work, take responsibility for the experiences in your life, see the rich lessons in it all, and let go of the painful experiences, you can easily fall back into disempowerment. It takes awareness and practice to reinforce the positive experiences and create new neuropathways to a vision of strong self-leadership.

I began to experience periods of awareness, surrender, peace, and bliss each time I moved across the country. Packing up all of my belongings so many times, I began to see the big picture of my life more and more with each move. However, until I went back and healed the parts of myself that were still groveling in disempowerment, I would get settled in to my new place and then, boom, there I was again. As the expression goes, no matter where you go, there you are. Anything that was not dealt with in my past would sneak up, triggering the old patterns of self-critical beliefs. The more I allowed the process, rather than sweeping uncomfortable feelings under the rug, and the more tools I gained for unlocking my mind's potential, the easier it became to clear out the clutter and begin to live in a more reverent way.

What if you look back and find the same patterns are repeating themselves? You may feel that everything you work toward falls

apart; you may find yourself in the same disempowering relationships, experiencing poor health, or just feeling complacent and
unmotivated. You may read this book and think that empowering
yourself is impossible because of all the evidence you have to the
contrary. I want to challenge you to begin believing you can break
the patterns no longer serving you. As you use the tools in this book,
you will gain the confidence to break free from those patterns and
create new ones. From a scientific standpoint, you can create real
change just by changing your thoughts, infusing into your conscious
and unconscious mind an "I can do it, I am enough, I am worthy"
mindset, and then taking small steps toward the change. You can
begin to compile evidence that you absolutely have all the tools,
mentors, resources, and intrinsic knowledge you need to unlock
your own true potential.

> *From a scientific standpoint, you can create real change just
> by changing your thoughts, infusing into your conscious and
> unconscious mind an "I can do it, I am enough, I am worthy"
> mindset, and then taking small steps toward the change.*

Once you gain a better understanding of how to program your mind
to embody a positive mindset, the natural progression is to take
the positively inspired action toward your vision. Having a positive
mindset naturally invokes positive action. I cover all the aspects of
vision building in Chapter 16. As you begin taking action toward
your vision, you will know by how you feel whether you are in a
disempowering action state or an unleashed action state.

WORK MODE

It is a common misconception that to be successful, you must push every day toward an aggressively mapped out goal, and that doing so must look and feel like hard work. I'm not suggesting that you shouldn't make goals and work toward them. I'm just suggesting that it doesn't have to *feel* difficult, so I am inviting you to be very aware of your thoughts and how your body feels as you work.

I have always had a very strong work ethic. My father, a retired Army master sergeant, taught me the value of hard work. There was always something to build or do on our property on top of the early mornings spent caring for the horses and other animals. I actually enjoyed digging post holes when we laid the fifty-acre fence line. I felt great satisfaction burning off all my pent-up emotions, holding the post-hole digger as high as possible in the air with all my strength, and slamming it into the hard dirt, grabbing as much as the digger would hold, pulling it up and out hundreds of times, and then smashing the heavy iron chiseled bar into the hole to break up the hard clay and rock. This was the summer I built my arm muscles and sported a tank top tan at the ripe age of twelve. I felt that summer that the mean kids at school wouldn't dare bother me now with those muscles!

I carried that work ethic with me, putting all my masculine energy into my work throughout my twenties, until I became more aware of myself and realized that this "work mode" energy didn't feel good— it felt like pushing. I realized I got into this work mode masculine energy each time I dove into a task, whether it be in my corporate work or cleaning house.

I wondered why I felt different when I was working versus when I was going for a walk in the woods. Why couldn't it all feel the same? I thought it was natural to have a hurried, pushing intensity while working. As I became more aware of my thoughts, I realized I kicked into competition mode when I worked.

When I really began to pay attention to how my body felt and what was going through my mind, I recognized a heaviness in my chest and that my thoughts were full of self-critical thoughts. When I dove into where this originated, I found that it went back to feelings of not being good enough when doing chores as a child. My stepmother was a perfectionist and my father often parented like a drill sergeant, so I would constantly be worried whether what I did was good enough for them. I carried this into my work life and took on the same perfectionist mentality toward everything I did. I found as I became more aware of the energy behind my work that my thoughts were self-critical and full of competing, judging, and comparing. I had been infusing all my work with a disempowering state. This is where most people remain stuck in the levels of competition, comparison, and judging toward self and others.

My suggestion here is to consider that work, whether it be your secular work or day-to-day tasks, can feel effortless. To lead yourself so that others will want to follow you, you have to unveil the core of whatever keeps you stuck in competing, comparing, and judging. The first step is becoming aware of your thoughts throughout the day. If you are constantly checking out what everyone else is doing, making judgments about the competition, and comparing what you are doing to what others are doing, you are in a disempowerment state. If you are striving, yearning and pushing constantly, you are not honoring the flow of abundance and cannot lead as intuitively. If you worry there isn't enough business to go around, you are missing out on accessing a more powerful flow of abundance and will have difficulty truly connecting with people authentically because distrust and doubt will constantly be lingering in the background of your mind. If you find yourself making judgmental remarks about others, if you find joy in gossip, if your self-talk is critical, and if you are constantly competing and judging yourself and others, then you are in the first story, disempowerment stages.

To lead yourself so that others will want to follow you, you have to unveil the core of whatever keeps you stuck in competing, comparing, and judging.

If you feel you are the only one who is getting it right, that your competition is doing it all wrong, that you are the best, and that there is nothing new to learn, you have not yet unleashed into your authentic leadership potential.

Are you triggered when you see others succeed? This is the most difficult stage to break because you must first be aware enough to realize you are in it. Just reading this chapter may wake you up and help you become more aware. Awareness can be the first step to your unleashing.

INTEGRITY

The first sign you are beginning to live your life in the second story of unleashing is through your integrity. This is where you begin to lead your own life, not as a reflection of what has happened to you, but by taking responsibility for your life, seeing the lessons in it all, and knowing what you deserve in your life, love, and work. You begin to develop a stronger sense of intuition and can begin to hear the still, quiet voice that answers when you ask a question. You no longer care what others are thinking about you, and you are no longer feeling competitive. You realize the power of your thoughts. You become very intentional about your language. You begin to recognize when you are comparing and judging, and you quickly make the shift to finding something you admire about yourself and others. You see your competition is living in their purpose and you have reverence for their journey, whether you feel you can do it better or not.

The "me versus them" mentality begins to melt away. You begin to feel a connection to others. There is a shift in your energy charge toward people in your social media newsfeed and toward people outside of your social circle. You are no longer triggered by people showing up and celebrating their lives. You celebrate them too. You are no longer emotionally charged by people who have different beliefs. You become more in alignment with your word and with your still, inner knowing, and you begin to rise into your voice. You no longer make choices based in need and lack or to compete with others. You are no longer willing to associate with or work for people who disempower you. You become very clear on what you will stand for in your relationships. You develop a stronger integrity for what is required to rise up into your higher purpose and to experience joy. You take all you learned in your first story and use it as fuel to unleash who you truly are.

Part of the integrity piece is scanning all areas of your life and putting what is out of balance in sync. This includes your physical, spiritual, and emotional health, current and past relationships, and how you spend your time. Typically, the best place to start is in your own health as outlined in Chapter 11. In the integrity stage, it is most beneficial to begin to set small goals and hold yourself accountable to them. For example, when I stopped getting up early in the mornings and found myself scrolling through social media at midnight, I knew I was out of sync with what I was being called to do. If I listened to my intuition, it would tell me to go to bed early and get up early so I could set intention for my day and accomplish more before my family woke. As I began getting up early every morning, it naturally empowered me, and I grew confidence, feeling a sense of accomplishment because I was being true to what I knew was necessary to juggle work and family.

Another important step is to get back into integrity in your relationships. This may mean having authentic conversations with people, past and present. Most people will live their entire lives without mending a relationship that has been a weight on their heart or speak their truth about how a relationship affected them, forgive, and move past it. They carry these circumstances around with them like pulling a cart full of luggage everywhere they go. When you can stand in your truth in your relationships, you are honoring yourself. This is the greatest gift to yourself and often to the other people involved.

The best way I have found to approach a touchy relationship is first to take 100 percent responsibility for your part. Then let the other person know, "I am sorry that I led you to believe that this was okay. In fact, when you do this, it makes me feel _____." (Or "In fact, when this happened, I _____.") "From now on, in order to be true to myself, _____." (Or "Going forward, what can we come up with together to make this a mutually satisfying relationship?") Some conversations will require you to take 100 percent responsibility for being out of integrity in some way. These conversations help move the relationship in whatever direction is necessary for both parties to live in their own truth and their own integrity.

The following exercise helps you acknowledge where you are out of integrity. This is not an opportunity to beat yourself up or to feel guilt or place blame in any way. If guilt or blame come up, make it an opportunity to forgive and let go. This is simply an inventory of your life. Simply state the facts and whatever step or steps come to mind. This exercise will best serve you if you use the following wording, "I acknowledge I have been out of integrity in my health by: _____, and I am committed to taking this step or steps to improve: _____."

INTEGRITY EXERCISE:

Where am I out of integrity in my health? What small, inspired action step can I take now to make a shift?

_____

_____

_____

_____

_____

Where am I out of integrity in my self-love? What small, inspired action step can I take now to make a shift?

_____

_____

_____

_____

_____

Where am I out of integrity in how I lead in my relationships? What small, inspired action step can I take now to make a shift?

_____

_____

_____

_____

_____

Where am I out of integrity with what I feel called to be? What small, inspired action step can I take now to make a shift?

_____

_____

_____

_____

_____

Where am I out of integrity with what I feel called to do? What small, inspired action step can I take now to make a shift?

_____

_____

_____

_____

_____

Where am I out of integrity in my spirituality? What small, inspired action step can I take now to make a shift?

_____

_____

_____

_____

Where am I out of integrity in my finances? What small, inspired action step can I take now to make a difference?

_____

_____

_____

_____

_____

Where am I out of integrity in honoring my time? What small, inspired action step can I take now to make a shift?

_____

_____

_____

_____

_____

Where am I out of integrity in having reverence for my journey? What small, inspired action step can I take now to make a shift?

_____

_____

_____

_____

_____

Where am I out of integrity in having reverence for others' journeys? What small, inspired action step can I take now to make a shift?

_____

_____

_____

_____

So what happens when you have a bad day or a bad week and fail miserably at showing up as your best self or manifesting something you have worked really hard toward? You may feel down for an entire month, or you may experience something that knocks you down for a while. This is a part of being human! Can you imagine if you never tried to stretch yourself outside of your comfort zone? Jack Canfield, *New York Times* best-selling author of *The Success Principles* and co-creator of the Chicken Soup for the Soul series, encourages us: "Don't worry about failures, worry about the chances you miss when you don't even try." He is the perfect example of never giving up. After getting rejected by 144 publishers, his first *Chicken Soup for the Soul* book was finally picked up by a small publisher and eventually that led to him becoming a *New York Times* best-selling author with more than 500 million copies of his books sold. Can you imagine being rejected 144 times? The key is to pick yourself back up, brush yourself off, and take small steps to getting back on track. One of the best movie lines of all time was spoken by Alfred in *Batman Begins*: "Why do we fall? So that we can learn to pick ourselves up." Never give up on yourself no matter how hard you fall. All it takes is acknowledging your responsibility in the situation, recommitting to the small, inspired action steps, and carrying them out with consistency. We all know, if we ask the deeper questions of ourselves, where we can take these small steps to lead ourselves to live more fulfilling lives.

As you prove to yourself that you can live in integrity with what you feel called to be and do, you will be empowered in your new, inspired action and grow confidence in yourself. Your creativity will deepen more and more. You will feel an ease in your work as you are in the flow of it. Your intuition will become your guide so you know when to move forward and when to hold off. It is not a constant pushing. You are in tune with what your body requires and have a knowing of what inspired action to take and when to take it. You move into surrender and letting go.

As you prove to yourself that you can live in integrity with what you feel called to be and do, you will be empowered in your new, inspired action and grow confidence in yourself.

From a scientific perspective, you have created new neuropathways in your brain and changed your perception of past trauma and failures. You have developed a deeper emotional intelligence so that you are no longer attached to the emotions that do not serve you. You no longer have to be in control because your intuition is driving the ship. You are willing to surrender to the process, the unveiling of your true authentic self. Now you will find more opportunities to forgive and let go. As you forgive yourself and others, you feel lighter and more joyful. You will move into a deeper understanding of your life. It is as if you have floated above your life and can see the rich lessons weaved into all of your experiences. All of this occurs in the unleashing stages of self-leadership.

As you become fully unleashed, you are in a better position to lead others because you naturally become more compassionate and altruistic. The focus is no longer on self. You are compelled to help others and make a mark on the world. The center focus of all you do and the person you are is cemented in reverence. This means you can understand the bigger picture of other people's lives and you do not get offended easily. You don't feel there is anything you have to forgive of anyone because you are able to tap into unconditional love where there is no judgment. You have a deep knowing that everyone is doing the best they can given their current awareness. When you lead your own life with reverence, you will experience gratitude, feel peaceful, and have more love and joy in your life. This is where ultimate intuition kicks in, and you will be pulled by a greater purpose. This is a state where everything becomes a creative act, and you are in the flow of true abundance.

CHAPTER 13

Leading With Intention

*A true leader has the confidence to stand alone, the courage to make
tough decisions, and the compassion to listen to the needs of others.
He does not set out to be a leader, but becomes one by the
equality of his actions and the integrity of his intent.*

— GENERAL DOUGLAS MACARTHUR

As outlined in the previous chapter, all leadership begins with self-
leadership. The next step is to infuse reverent intention into leading
others. *Your Story of Intention* as outlined in Chapters 2, 3, and 4 can
determine how effective you will be as a leader and how you will feel
leading yourself and others. The old way of leading, with competition at the forefront, and in many cases, using shaming, reward/
punishment, and a survival-of-the-fittest mentality has taken us
down a spiral of government corruption, corporate greed, fear-based
religion, authoritarian parenting, and one-size-fits-all academic systems. The new form of leadership calls for us to appeal to people's
intrinsic reward systems. As author and speaker John C. Maxwell
says: "Leaders become great not because of their power, but because
of their ability to empower others." People want to feel empowered
in their work. Empowerment is the greatest intrinsic motivator.

Leading by empowering people can help grow revenue. If you focus on growing people, your bottom line will grow exponentially and with less effort.

Leading by empowering people can help grow revenue. If you focus on growing people, your bottom line will grow exponentially and with less effort.

In all my years working for corporations, I have experienced both great and poor examples of leadership. I also got to experience leading others in various capacities. The most rewarding experience in my corporate days was when I owned a medical services company. I managed various personalities, but for me, the most interesting stretch was managing clinicians as a non-clinical person. I allowed them to lead themselves in their own talents and capabilities, while supporting them. In hindsight, I realized my partner and I were able to attract highly experienced talent because of the heart-centered vision we built the company on and our ability to paint a picture of how they fit into it. We built a patient-first operation and grew despite a saturated market because of the intention we infused into every interaction with our patients and customers.

What does it mean to lead with intention? The intention I write about here is an intrinsic intention that resides within, where ultimate intuition and pure creativity flows. Chapter 7 on intention and language outlines the power of tapping into this force field. Leading with intention calls for harmony, collaboration, connection, and reverent intention: reverent leaders serve with integrity, let go of past failures, and bring out the best in people. They lead more intuitively and foster harmony in the workplace. They are also strong communicators and can effortlessly ignite the intrinsic rewards within people. Reverent leaders have ignited their personal stories and can use story as an inspirational tool. They lead with honesty and transparency and give praise freely. They show up consistently in joy to serve their teams, and it is their goal to cultivate other leaders. If they make a mistake, they do not hide it or cover it up. They own it. Reverent leaders have a willingness to collaborate and encourage other leaders to rise up into their gifts and talents.

> *Reverent leaders have a willingness to collaborate and encourage other leaders to rise up into their gifts and talents.*

You may notice that most advertisements and commercials appeal to the second story that people live, the part of us that competes and compares. Most corporations are teetering between stories of competition and comparison and integrity and empowerment. Infusing the higher-level intentions of understanding, compassion, and reverence into your mission statement, and into the way you serve and lead, will drastically shift everything and likely lead to growth. When your story is infused with reverent language that appeals to people's unconscious, intrinsic reward systems, you will find that it is easier to attract business. When people feel honored, cared for, and supported, your employee retention will skyrocket.

How can leaders and corporations make this shift? The answer starts within. As I pointed out before, while most believe leadership is the

act of leading others, actually conscious leaders are experts at leading themselves and activating self-leadership within others. They
do the work necessary on themselves and in their personal lives so
they can show up consistently in joy to serve their teams and cultivate other leaders. When there are roadblocks or setbacks, they are
fully transparent with their teams, and together, they come up with
solutions. These leaders have not only embodied their visions for
their personal lives full of joy, peace, good health, connection, and
abundance, but they carry that over into their work. No division
exists between their personal and work lives in terms of the positive
calibration in which they show up. The best leaders are invested in
their own personal growth, and they lead balanced, fulfilled lives,
encouraging team members to do the same.

Some question this approach, saying it is too soft or if they lead in
a way that fosters work/life balance, they will not attract hard workers. Actually, the opposite is true. If leaders set the stage for integrity
toward their altruistic missions and hold their teams and customers
in the highest regard, they will begin to embody what it takes to
become reverent leaders. Naturally, they will attract more devoted
employees because they are pulled daily by a bigger purpose and
vision. They will develop stronger intuitive insight to lead themselves and their teams toward that vision. Their teams will begin to
embody the heart-centered vision as it becomes the story of how the
corporation runs on a daily basis.

By leading from a higher intentional state in the third story of reverence, you will find that people show up who want to serve your
mission. Here is where the synchronicities occur as you tap into the
flow of abundance. This new way of leadership is required for our

global shift toward honoring others' gifts and talents and allowing them to shine in their own leadership capabilities. Everyone has the right to live in what they feel called to do and feel the intrinsic rewards that come with living in their gifts.

A MILLION-DOLLAR MORNING

Putting intrinsic intention aside, what about the daily habits of leaders, the extrinsic intention that leaders carry out in their day-to-day actions? The way leaders start their days can set the stage for how their entire lives play out. It is no secret that the most successful leaders get up early in the morning. The CEO of Apple, Tim Cook, gets up at 3:45 a.m. to go through email, exercise, and grab a coffee before settling in to his work day. Oprah Winfrey gets up naturally between 6:00 and 6:20 a.m. to walk her dogs, indulge in a chai tea or cappuccino, exercise, and meditate before eating breakfast or diving into work. Disney CEO Bob Iger gets up at 4:30 a.m. to read. Square CEO Jack Dorsey is up at 5:30 a.m. jogging. News anchor Ann Curry gets up at 3:45 a.m. as well. Longtime *Vogue* editor Anna Wintour is on the tennis court by 6:00 a.m. Early morning routines and success go hand in hand.

What would it look like for you to begin going to bed earlier, getting up just thirty minutes earlier, and working your way to getting up between 5 and 6 a.m.? What more would you accomplish? When I began writing this book, I found between juggling coaching and children that I wasn't getting very far in the writing process. I made the commitment to my coach to get up three days per week at 5:30 a.m. to write. This worked for several months. When I woke up, it was still dark out. I began by standing out in my backyard

looking up at the pitch-dark sky, breathing in the cool air, and setting my intention with gratitude and prayer. Then I would shift into
a light mindfulness meditation, focusing on my breath, grounding
myself, and reciting my *I am* statements. Having that extra hour or
so before my children woke up was pivotal in building momentum
for my book.

I found in the final months of writing my book that I required
longer stretches to write, so I made the commitment to begin writing a few hours on the weekends. In the few months I reverted back
to night-owl routine, I found I missed that time to connect and set
my intention for the day. For me, those early mornings before my
family woke up were a time to connect with myself and become an
instrument for the spirit to work through me to bring my vision
to life. I realized I had to nourish myself and my creativity before
my sweet little ones woke up. I went back to getting up early every
day in the final stretches of editing this book and made the commitment to myself to continue the morning routine. Rising early
in the mornings, I am the leader of my day. I am in control of the
intention infused into my day, and I can set the tone for the energy
of my day by waking earlier.

What if you are not a morning person? The first question I would
ask is, "Are you in integrity with your vision for your life? Are you
being true to the creative nudges? Are you at peak health? Are you
showing up as a leader in your field?" If you answered yes to these
questions, then no worries, sleep in. If not, it may be time to reconsider your schedule. Even if it is not an earlier morning routine, ask
yourself, "Without sacrificing my personal life and health, how can
I schedule time in my day to honor the greater vision of my life?"
This includes self-leadership of your body, your spiritual and emotional health, your relationships, and your mission.

MINDFULNESS

Another important aspect of intention is awareness of the present moment. Mindfulness is defined by the *Merriam-Webster Dictionary* as, "The practice of maintaining a nonjudgmental state of heightened or complete awareness of one's thoughts, emotions, or experiences on a moment-to-moment basis." Mindfulness meditation increases the thickness in the prefrontal cortex and parietal lobes of the brain associated with attention control. It also increases gray matter (the tissue containing neurons where all synapses are) in parts of the brain related to learning, memory, self-awareness, and compassion. All research points to practicing mindfulness as a way for CEOs to build resilience, boost emotional intelligence, enhance creativity, improve relationships, boost optimism, and help with focus. Overall, beginning your day with deep breathing, breathing in your true essence and exhaling any worry or fear, can set the tone for a grounded, balanced day.

> *All research points to practicing mindfulness as a way for CEOs to build resilience, boost emotional intelligence, enhance creativity, improve relationships, boost optimism, and help with focus.*

Other studies suggest that employees benefit from leaders who practice mindfulness. The leader showing up more grounded and calm sets the tone for the day's energy. Employees of leaders practicing mindfulness report feeling less emotional drain, better work/life balance, and improved job performance.

How can you begin incorporating mindfulness into your daily routine? Try starting your day with a mindfulness meditation three days per week and reflect on how it affects the rest of your day. Then begin weaving in a mindfulness session before or after lunch and before bed. If you pray, make these sessions a part of your daily routine. Connect with your breath and be in the still, quiet space for a while. This is the calm, peaceful state where you can ask a question and receive the answer. As you become more grounded, connected, and focused, you will be more productive, feel more balanced, and become more intuitive.

MINDFUL LEADER SCHEDULE:

Monday

Wake: _____ Routine: _____

_____

Tuesday

Wake: _____ Routine: _____

_____

Wednesday

Wake: _____ Routine: _____

_____

Thursday

Wake: _____ Routine: _____

_____

Friday

Wake: _____ Routine: _____

_____

Saturday

Wake: _____ Routine: _____

_____

Sunday

Wake: _____ Routine: _____

_____

MINDFULNESS AT WORK

What about incorporating mindfulness into the workplace? What would that look like for your team? According to the Mindfulness Initiative in the United Kingdom, "Over the last forty years, mindfulness practices have been combined with modern psychological theory and developed into a secular training that has been the subject of thousands of scientific trials."

This research proves that employees in mindfulness work environments report less stress, longer concentration, and improved ability to focus. Receiving insight from your team on how you can begin incorporating daily mindfulness would be a start. It may be beneficial to bring in a mindfulness coach and create a mindfulness space. Some corporations delegate specific inside or outside spaces where people can bring yoga mats and take the mental break they need to rejuvenate for the rest of their day. Just taking ten to twenty minutes a day to sit at your workspace, close your eyes with your feet grounded, and your hands by your side can improve mental focus and reduce stress. Innovations Academy, a K-8 charter school in San Diego, California, implements mindfulness sessions twice daily into its schedule. Imagine if every family, every school, and every corporation were to integrate a mindfulness practice into its culture?

FREEDOM

Dr. Seuss painted the picture of micromanagement perfectly in his book, *Did I Ever Tell You How Lucky You Are?* with the watchers (managers) growing in number until the whole town was just watching the one person with an actual job—the bee watcher.

No one wants to be micromanaged. People are more productive when they are free to do their jobs.

People can be just as productive in less time if they are included in planning, have regular check-ins, are offered support, have clear deadlines, and are free to perform. I personally believe in a four-day work-week and four-day school-week; however, I know it is not always possible for every line of work or as a set schedule. If it is not possible for your corporation, what about full or partial work-from-home days for your top-performing employees or as a rotation for everyone? As long as the work is completed and the parameters and support systems are clear, does it matter when and where the work takes place? Within reason, is it possible for your employees to create their own work hours? For people with families, this flexibility may provide a much-needed afternoon off with their children. Some employees would jump at the option to come in at 6 a.m. to be done by 2 p.m. As long as your team members play a part in the strategy, and there is a mutual agreement on responsibilities, providing more time flexibility for your team improves rapport and work/life balance. Employees who are honored in this way become more invested in your vision.

WORKSPACE

Rather than cubicles, some organizations like CBRE in Los Angeles allow their employees to choose their daily workspaces, including couches, collaboration rooms, or acoustically-treated, single-person glass enclaves. Get feedback from your team members on how they can create more freedom in their workspaces. Is it possible to sit outside and work at a picnic bench? Can high-performing employees go to the local coffee shop down the road to work? Can team members, under appropriate leadership, work on a project at one of the team member's homes? Providing options for people on where and how they want to work will improve employee satisfaction and retention. The key is to provide a structure that cultivates commitment, planning, and integrity, while allowing your team the freedom to figure out how to carry out the work.

FEEDBACK AND COLLABORATION

Another great way to create an atmosphere of reverence in your workplace is to honor the team's input. Ask for feedback and allow for collaboration. Provide an anonymous feedback link, offer a confidential comment box, or use Survey Monkey and bring those insights to discuss at your weekly or monthly meetings. How do we know how we are doing if we aren't asking? Some of the best ideas come from our teams who are down in the trenches with the clients and facing the daily challenges. Honor their feedback and use it as fuel for collaboration, allowing the natural flow of creativity to come forth.

Honor their feedback and use it as fuel for collaboration, allowing the natural flow of creativity to come forth.

Dr. Emoto's research on the power of language and intention showed a profound difference between the water crystallization evoked by the words "Let's do it," versus simply "Do it." The "Do it" water did not form crystals at all. The "Let's do it" water crystals formed into beautiful snowflakes. Collaboration is powerful! If your intention is to ignite leaders in your corporation, creating an atmosphere of collaboration using positive language will help cultivate their courage to rise into their gifts and talents.

ENROLLING YOUR TEAM WITH VISION

When you are clear on your short and long-term vision for the company and communicate it well to your team, you are one step ahead in gaining their commitment to help fulfill it. What language are you using at meetings and in your daily interactions to help keep your team connected to the vision?

Visualization can also be a powerful tool in creating more commitment from your team members. Walk them through a visualization showing how this vision will impact your target customers and how, in turn, the growth will impact them. Discover what drives your team members and find ways to cater to their key motivating factors. Find out what their visions are and show how you can weave their visions into the company's long-term vision. Allow them to outline their goals and visions and suggest how they fit into the company. Research shows that visioning and goal setting cause the release of dopamine, the happiness hormone, in the brain. Creating that experience together solidifies the team. Having team members create individual vision boards for their workspaces, and together, create a company vision board that is seen and experienced daily further activates the parts of their brains that will emotionalize the future rewards of working together as a team.

> *Discover what drives your team members and find ways to cater to their key motivating factors.*

CELEBRATION

Teams that celebrate together, stay together. Dopamine runs high when there is celebration. This motivating hormone is emitted by the brain when goals are achieved. Breaking the vision down into small, achievable pieces, and then celebrating each step in the series of goals creates a sense of personal accomplishment and team camaraderie. It is crucial to create new goals continuously while on the way to achieving the larger ones, so goals are reached and celebrated consistently. This process produces a steady pace of dopamine-producing celebrations. Real celebration is key. It could come in small forms of appreciation like a celebratory email or pizza Friday. Celebration creates an atmosphere of fun for your team.

Teams that celebrate together, stay together.

FUN AT WORK

The question I've always asked myself is, "Why aren't we having more fun at work?" Bright HR, a cloud-based human resources firm, found in its "It Pays to Play" study that having fun at work reduced sick days and contributed to better health and wellbeing. Seventy-nine percent of its millennial participants reported that having fun at work is important, and 44 percent believed it stimulated a better work ethic. Fifty-six percent of fifty-five to sixty year olds felt the same way, while only 14 percent believed it stimulated a better work ethic. I speculate that these results reflect the deep-seated belief that hard work should feel like hard work.

How can you bring fun into your personal life *and* incorporate it into your work environment now? Typically, a leadership team sets the tone for how much fun is to be had at work. Working in corporate, I noticed that, overall, the salespeople had more time freedom than those who worked in the office. They had the space to drive around in their cars and practice mindfulness, whether they realized it or not. They were in charge of the interactions they had and did not have the pressure to comply with whatever energy permeated the home base. How can we, as leaders, create a more mindful, light-hearted environment at the home base, while keeping productivity up?

The best way to find out is to ask. Plan a *fun* meeting, and ask your team that question. You will be surprised what comes back. Here are some ideas: office night-outs, morning huddle with a work agenda and something fun planned, joke of the day, dance-offs, relay race, office pet, dress-down Fridays, family potluck in the park, health fair, bingo, raffles, wellbeing massage days, access to an elliptical machine in the office, birthday celebrations, contests, karaoke, and fundraising. See what your team comes up with!

EMPLOYEE SATISFACTION AND RETENTION

It is common knowledge that people are not as motivated by bonuses as they once were. Research highlighted in a Payscale Salary Survey white paper suggested in 2015 and 2016 that data collected on 501,796 workers showed that, overall, employees want to feel their gifts and talents are appreciated and that they have a future in their company.

Here are two $1,000,000 questions to ponder: How are you showcasing the vision for your company and your team's gifts and talents to improve employee retention? Better yet, how are you enrolling your employees in your vision and assisting them in visualizing themselves in that vision? With more emphasis on work/life balance and personal happiness, it is imperative for a leader to create an environment where people are moved intrinsically and feel like they belong and are valued.

When it comes to employee satisfaction, feeling appreciated now ranks higher than receiving bonuses, and if your employees perceive the company will stick around for a long time, it's likely your employee retention will improve, if you also remember to show your gratitude for them being there. There are myriads of ways to show your employees they are valued. Besides asking them for feedback, offering them freedom, including fun in their work environment, and unexpected time off, another way to show appreciation is by verbally praising them specifically on how they handled a challenge or led a project. Personalized praise in front of the team can have a profound effect. Team-building events, experiential surprises, allowing them to make decisions, and letting them in on the planning of company strategy are equally helpful.

With more emphasis on work/life balance and personal happiness, it is imperative for a leader to create an environment where people are moved intrinsically and feel like they belong and are valued.

A neat app called YouEarnedIt offers employees the ability to give each other praise and appreciation for a job well done. Just as we have languages of love, we also have languages of appreciation as outlined in *The 5 Languages of Appreciation in the Workplace* by Gary Chapman and Paul White. This book provides an assessment to help identify the most beneficial ways to give positive feedback to your team members based on their "appreciation language." Taking an interest in how each employee prefers to be praised can create a more positive dynamic work relationship. Imagine if this question was asked during every onboarding process.

MILLENNIALS, HAPPINESS, AND LEARNING

By 2025, 75 percent of the nation's workforce will be led by millennials. As visionaries, this young, vibrant population values work/life balance and learning over anything else. An Eventbrite survey showed that millennials prefer experiences to material possessions, with 69 percent believing they can connect with others, build community, and impact the world through the experiences. If you are leading an organization of millennials, this is something to keep in mind when you think about how to show your appreciation. Millennials may value a team-building rock-climbing adventure, a fundraising event, or an exciting new project they can learn from and collaborate on over an impersonal Starbucks gift card. Happiness in the workplace for them includes having freedom and knowing they are appreciated. Millennials require verbal expressions of appreciation more often than generations before them. They thrive on a positive work environment, and according to Gallup statistics, millennials value opportunities to grow and learn most of all. The best leaders of millennials will discover the millennials' vision, then align their business strategies to allow their younger workers to stretch themselves and showcase their creativity. Job satisfaction and employee retention will skyrocket if you are constantly providing millennials with the opportunity for professional development and to add to their learning experiences.

The best leaders of millennials will discover the millennials' vision, then align their business strategies to allow their younger workers to stretch themselves and showcase their creativity.

Overall, no matter the demographic and age of your teams, leading with the intention of reverence shifts the focus from growing your company to growing people. Celebrate them every day. Praise them in public. Offer constructive feedback in private. Allow them to be the creative force behind their work and have freedom to choose how they work. Build them up with a joyful work environment and encourage them to shine in their gifts and talents. Lead yourself in a way that embodies reverence; this will naturally overlap into the way you lead others. This new way of leadership is necessary to accommodate the conscious shift occurring on a global scale.

LEADERSHIP INSPIRATIONS:

What shifts are you inspired to make as a leader?

_____

_____

_____

_____

_____

_____

_____

_____

_____

_____

_____

_____

_____

_____

CHAPTER 14

Tapping Into Pure Creativity

The fact is that creativity is not born in the head. It's not even of this world. It is received as a gift from beyond, delivered as a rush or wave of inspiration. It is a love story—will and action merging with imagination, feeling, and being.

– BARNET BAIN

You are meant to live creatively—every moment. The story of your life is infused with purpose, and part of your purpose is to express yourself and to feel alive. Anytime you feel stuck or stagnant, it is because you are not honoring your creativity, your inner child, your voice, or your vision. In a world of hurriedness, busyness, achieving, striving, yearning, comparing, how can you stay true to the creative essence of who you are? Most people wake up and immediately get on their phones or turn on the TV. They start their day in reaction mode—reacting to the stimuli coming their way, rather than tapping into spirit and connecting with the source of all creativity. As a mother, if I get up before my two daughters, I am able to start the day by connecting within, becoming one with nature, and connecting in gratitude through prayer and meditation. We create the foundation of our day through our morning routine. Imagine starting your day by going outside, taking deep breaths, and taking in all the beautiful creation of the day. You begin to feel more alive. Then close your eyes and imagine a bright beam of light connecting you to the source of that aliveness through the crown of your head and grounding you into the core of the earth. Our creative expression can flow through this connection throughout the day. Otherwise, we are in a reactive state to everything and everyone around us, rather than a state of responsiveness, leaning into the creative flow.

You are meant to live creatively—every moment. The story of your life is infused with purpose, and part of your purpose is to express yourself and to feel alive.

Being in creative flow does not mean you have to be an artist, musician, writer, film maker, designer, etc. There is creative flow in everything you do throughout the day.

Embody the notion that every action is a creative act and an energy flows through everything that we do. Imagine a creative flow of energy present in a chore as simple as doing the dishes. Start by emptying your mind of all thoughts and place intention on the present moment. As you fill the sink with soap and water, you explore all five senses. You can hear and see the water flowing out. You notice the creative expression of each bubble; you place your hands into the water and feel its comfortable warmth; you watch the flow of water cascading down; the aroma of the dish detergent fills your senses—you take note of how your breath feels entering and exiting your nose. Your shoulders become relaxed and you fall into slower breathing as you intentionally place each dish into the water. You create a rhythm with each swirl of your sponge on the dish. When you hit a tough spot, rather than working against it, you use rhythm, flow, and intentional power to whisk the food away, setting it free from the dish. As you rinse the particles and soap off of the dish, you admire the clean, sparkling, glistening dish and place it carefully and intentionally into the dish rack. You continue on with every dish, pan, and cutlery piece, washing rhythmically and intentionally. Having no thoughts flooding your mind, you feel the flow of intentional cleaning for each piece. You honor the process. You notice your breath has become deeper and slower, and you feel connected with all your senses as you complete the washing, rinsing, and stacking of the dishes.

Once you have stimulated all five senses, you can tap into your sixth sense...your intuition, the flow of creativity and inspiration. Imagine a flow of creative energy cascading down into the crown of your head, through your heart, and out through your fingertips. Every motion is intentional and connected. Now infuse that with gratitude. Gratitude that you had food to eat, gratitude that you have dishes to wash, a home, and a family to feed (if relevant to you). Gratitude for the people who created the dishes and the soap. Gratitude for running water, etc. You get the picture.

Imagine doing this with every action all day, being fully present and feeling the flow of creativity and present-moment awareness into the action—folding laundry, weeding the garden, cooking, cleaning, tidying up, going for a walk, taking a shower, combing your hair, making the bed, engaging in conversation, and in your daily work tasks. Infuse the action with the intention of gratitude and be completely in a present state. Notice how the action activates all six senses—touch, taste, sight, sound, smell, and intuitive flow of inspiration. Now carry that intention into your writing, your leadership, your parenting, your love relationship, and all you do in creating something new.

DAILY ACTION CREATIVITY:

Journal below how you can begin infusing creativity into daily actions:

_____

_____

_____

_____

_____

When we discover that we have access to the intuitive flow of creativity and inspiration in the core of who we are and in everything we do, we experience a major shift in our perception of our lives and the world. We begin to feel more alive and can access pure creativity from that aliveness. Howard Thurman describes this best: "Don't ask what the world needs. Ask what makes you come alive and go do it. Because what the world needs is more people who have come alive." When we can become more aware and conscious of what makes us feel more alive and we allow inspiration to flow through our bodies, we become vessels for a world-transforming message. This message could come in the way of infusing a story into your business to better connect with your clients or customers. It could come as the still, quiet voice that guides the conscious parenting of your children. It could come as a speaking or coaching platform, as a film or a book. It could come as nudges to give and serve or to take better care of our earth. It may come in the way of revamping how you lead in your work, and in your relationships. The flow of creativity is always there and can be accessed by connecting to the source of that aliveness.

> *When we discover that we have access to the intuitive flow of creativity and inspiration in the core of who we are and in everything we do, we experience a major shift in our perception of our lives and the world.*

You may experience periods where this flow of creativity and inspiration is stagnant. Writing this book, there were periods when I felt stuck—the words would not flow. My clients experience the same thing throughout their creative journeys. It can feel frustrating when you get up at five-thirty in the morning to write or block off time on a Saturday afternoon to write and nothing comes or it takes a long time to get into the flow. I began to realize that creative expression ebbs and flows and is largely dependent on the vessel—my body. In weeks where I was working out and eating well, the inspiration flowed more freely. On the rare occasion when I partook of sugar, I felt a block in my body and experienced brain fog. If unfinished business needed to be dealt with in my relationships, I felt a block in my body. I began to discover that I had to keep my vessel clean and clear of emotions that do not serve me. And I had to keep my body in tip-top shape to experience the flow of inspiration more easily. The most profound realization for me was when I tapped into embodying spirit—in a fully reverent state, the muse would take over.

Whether I was speaking, coaching, or writing, it flowed through me as if I were merely a scribe. I was not the source of it. I found that the more deeply I connected spiritually, and to being an instrument of a message bigger than me, the easier it was to get out of my own way and tap into pure creativity.

I began to ask myself, "How can I tap into this creative process faster and more easily?" The answer seemed so simple. *Connect with your breath.* The root of the word "inspire" is the Latin word *inspirare*, meaning "to breathe" or "blow into." Inspire (v.) in Middle English was also used to mean "breathe or put life or spirit into the human body; impart reason to a human soul."

By connecting with our breath, we connect with our spirit, our life force, and the source of all creativity.

WRITING

Before writing, I made a habit of scanning my body first to determine whether there was any block to the flow. I began connecting with my breath, unloading all thoughts, and feeling the flow of energy through my body. Sometimes I was just too much in my head, so to open up the gates of inspiration, I would practice deep breathing and go into prayer and meditation. Sometimes I would read, watch, or listen to something that helped me drop into my heart and feel the pure connection in spirit. Often, just setting my intention on becoming an instrument of healing and transformation, I could more easily shift into the creative flow.

If you try these exercises, you will know there is a release because you will feel it. You may experience immense gratitude felt through your heart, your eyes may well up in tears, you may experience a blissful joy or a shift, like a feeling of relief or a belief of strong renewed faith that you can do this. Often, you may instantly receive a flow of words that come so quickly you cannot type or write them out fast enough. At the very least, a sense of quiet will come over you, and you can then write better with keener focus. The important thing is to start writing immediately, even if you aren't sure what to write about. Write what comes to mind, and just keep placing your fingers on the keys or your pen to the paper until it flows through you.

The American novelist Louis L'Amour said: "Start writing, no matter what. The water does not flow until the faucet is turned on." You will know that bit of inspiration has reached the end when you stop writing. You can go through these exercises again and again to keep going in a long stretch of writing.

TAPPING INTO CREATIVE FLOW

You can tap into the creative flow by first connecting with your breath and then allowing yourself to daydream and receive the downloads. I personally ask for the downloads throughout the day, and they come, but not necessarily when I am sitting down to write. You can receive inspiration in nature, while in the shower, or while driving.

Have you ever wondered why inspiration comes at such times? While in nature, we tend to be more connected with our breath, the present moment, and everything around us. Being more present and in nature, we experience the basic core of who we are and the essence of planet earth. We and the earth are living, breathing nature. The same life force that flows through the earth flows through us. When we connect with nature, we experience the core of life's force and there inspiration can flow. While in the shower, the flow of the water pouring over our bodies puts us in the present moment where creativity flows. Scientifically speaking, we are experiencing more peaceful, daydream states because our alpha brain wave state is in higher gear and the logical, thinking state of beta brain wave is not as active. We are also away from all the typical distractions. Driving in our car, we may arrive at our home and have no memory of how we got there. This is because the unconscious part of our brains has programmed that route and our conscious mind is free to daydream.

Exercise is also a valuable tool in stimulating your creative expression. Research on the effects of exercise on the brain shows that aerobic activity actually increases the size of our hippocampus, the part of the brain we use to imagine the future and where ideas are created.

When you are in pure creativity, you are embodying third story reverence. You fully surrender to the process, and you typically feel at peace. A flow of inspiration moves through you. You feel confident in what you are working on. When you scan your body, there are no blocks, nothing separating you from the creative space. You feel whole and complete. You are tapped into ultimate intuition. Minimal thinking is required. You are using the parts of your brain where creativity, connection, and feel-good emotions originate. Your body may be tired, but you are running on creative fuel, so you feel energized. Here is where you feel most connected as an instrument for the creative spirit to flow through you.

No matter what you are doing, infuse the flow of creativity into it. Infuse every word, every action in the joy of the present moment. Whether folding laundry, painting a picture, leading a meeting, coaching, having a conversation with a loved one, writing your book or screenplay, dancing, or playing with your children, there is a flow of energy, and you become deliberate with every word, every stroke of the paintbrush, every movement, every playful action because you are fully immersed in the present moment and connected to the source of the inspiration's flow. Here is where time naturally passes, yet you feel no time has passed. It feels like everything is moving in slow motion because you are slowing down your perception of it from the logical, linear space to the creative, non-linear space.

Creativity and connection are one. When you feel disconnected, your creativity is blocked. Disconnection could occur in your relationships, your health, your emotions, and spirit. Disconnection from your vision can also hinder creativity, as you begin to forget what stimulated your creativity in the first place. Barnet Bain, an award-winning motion picture producer, director, and creativity expert, reminds us in *The Book of Doing and Being: Rediscovering Creativity in Life, Love, and Work*: "When we make contact with what matters, creative expression comes unimpeded from our deepest self." When you feel deeply connected to others, your higher self, your vision, and in Spirit, then inspired creativity naturally unfolds. Reconnecting to what drives you intrinsically will respark your creative musings as you get out of your own way and focus on your life's meaning and purpose.

Reconnecting to what drives you intrinsically will respark your creative musings as you get out of your own way and focus on your life's meaning and purpose.

CULTIVATING CREATIVITY

Here are ten keys for cultivating creativity:

1. **Feel Worthy, Confident:** The greatest block to creative flow is the feeling of unworthiness and being "not good enough." Comparing yourself to others is the death of creative expression. If you are constantly in the space of comparison, you are not honoring how you are made and how you are meant to express yourself.

2. **Be an Instrument:** The quickest way to tap into your creative flow is to ask to be an instrument. Realize that what comes through you is not from you. Become at one with your breath. Then allow the message, the ideas, the words, the art, the business structure, or the story to flow through you.

3. **Feel Complete:** Create a list of what makes you feel complete. For most, this sense of completeness is strengthened by their strong connection with family and friends, a deep spiritual connection, or a sense of belonging within a community. Whatever your source of feeling completeness, call upon it as you are creating.

4. **Feel the Joy:** Focus on what brings you joy. Wayne Dyer said, "Doing what you love is the cornerstone to having abundance in your life." To tap into your fullest creative potential, release and let go of anything that does not align with joy. Let go of expectation. Let go of your perception of lack, and instead, fill up that space with joy and passion.

5. **Feel the Freedom of Letting Go:** If you are still holding on to anything, let it go and forgive. Even if it is difficult to forgive, write a forgiveness letter and send the energy of forgiveness. Say over and over, "I forgive you," until you

feel, little by little, you have released whatever it is. This opens up the space for your true essence and creativity to shine through.

6. **Feel the Support:** Call upon loved ones. Imagine the people you most deeply love or who most deeply love you. Bring their faces, their essence, into your heart, and feel the joy that comes over you.

7. **Be the Stillness:** To be in the creative space, your mind must quiet down. It is important to shift into the stillness of your mind and be fully present in the moment. For the flow to occur, shift from the logical, thinking, doing mind into your reverent being state. How do you do this? By grounding yourself with your feet on the floor or sitting in a comfortable position. Begin by breathing deeply and holding each breath for two to three seconds before exhaling. Visualize grounding yourself and unloading thoughts from your mind. Visualize replacing the thoughts and busyness with stillness—whatever stillness means for you. Be the stillness. One of my clients found she could better hold herself accountable and settle into her writing by making an appointment with Jesus to write. She embodied the stillness of his presence and just wrote. She began showing up for her writing with a different energy. It shifted from "having" to write to "getting" to write. By discovering your source of stillness, you can embody your creative expression more fully. In this space, thoughts of uncertainty and doubt melt away as the creativity takes over.

8. **Find Your Intrinsic Motivation:** Detach from the outcome and find your intrinsic motivation. Here is where the Law of Attraction comes in. Working with your coach, you can create a vision for the outcome of your book, your

business, or your project. You can paint the picture of what that looks like, extrinsically, in the form of financial gain, personal satisfaction, recognition, and most importantly, the impact it will make. However, the key is letting go of the outcome and connecting to your intrinsic motivation. Why are you creating this? What is your intention? What within you drives you to express this idea? Become the instrument for this message.

9. **Honor the Ebb and Flow of the Process:** Allow for space to create. It takes time for creation to come forth. Sometimes, you have to research and marinate ideas before you create. Honor the creative ebb and flow of the process.

10. **Allow the Rising:** Just do it. Take action. The creative expression is already there. The book is already written. The film is already made. The hobby is already ignited. The business is already launched. The idea is already out there. It is just a matter of standing in the creative vision, taking action, and allowing the rising to occur.

The key is letting go of the outcome and connecting to your intrinsic motivation. Why are you creating this? What is your intention? What within you drives you to express this idea? Become the instrument for this message.

CREATIVITY EXERCISE:

What do I feel called to express in my creativity?

_____

_____

_____

When do I feel most creative?

_____

_____

_____

What inspired action steps can I take toward honoring my creativity?

_____

_____

_____

_____

_____

CHAPTER 15

Being in the Flow of Abundance

*I am now surrounded by an ocean of wealth and I
draw from this ocean all I need.*

– JOHN ASSARAF

People are always asking me, "How do I take what I want to do and create abundance from it?" My answer is that you cannot create abundance. Abundance is an inside job, the inner workings behind the scenes. Abundance is the fuel that makes you feel alive and free. There is a flow of abundance, so the key is to know how to connect to it. Intention plays a large role in making the connection. If you choose intention toward money and material gain only, the abundance will wear out. You can put all the intention you want toward what you want to attract into your life, but if you are just in it for yourself, anything you intend will eventually lose momentum. You will experience high highs and low lows. You will find yourself constantly having to remotivate yourself, and nothing you build and create will be good enough. You will be stuck in striving and yearning for more and more, while intrinsically feeling unfulfilled. Sound familiar?

Abundance is an inside job, the inner workings behind the scenes.

If you choose intention toward serving in some way, you can tap into the flow of abundance and gain energy. To experience true abundance, I suggest first shifting how you view the Law of Attraction. The Law of Attraction is based on placing your intention on receiving something and thereby receiving it—it's for you alone. The Law of Attraction focuses on changing your thoughts and beliefs and keeping your energy in high vibes and positivity to better attract what you want. Does it work? For some, absolutely! However, there is more to it. First of all, the planning and action pieces are missing. Secondly, in the basic philosophy of the Law of Attraction, the final destination is yourself. In the universe, there is no final destination. Everything in the universe has an ebb and flow, a giving and a receiving. Abundance works in the same way. There is a giving and a receiving in abundance. Abundance is a fuel that works and moves through you, not to you.

If you choose intention toward serving in some way, you can tap into the flow of abundance and gain energy.

How do you go from the hamster wheel of striving and yearning to simply being in the flow of abundance? First, let's define true abundance. True abundance is living in joy, freedom, and great health in body, mind, and spirit and having enough to bless others. As defined by Wikipedia, an abundant life signifies a contrast to feelings of lack, emptiness, and dissatisfaction, and such feelings may motivate a person to seek the meaning and a change in their life.

SEVEN COMPONENTS OF TRUE ABUNDANCE

To be in the flow of abundance, I invite you to start from within. Here are seven components of true abundance:

1. Abundance begins with your own self-love and your self-worth beliefs: When you honor your body and your spiritual and emotional health, you become a strong vessel for abundance to flow through. If you are holding onto things from the past, they will block the flow. If you are not honoring who you truly are and choosing not to listen when you are being called in various ways to love and care for yourself, your vessel will be weak and it will be nearly impossible to tap into the flow of abundance. As you develop a reverence for yourself, your ability to be in the flow of abundance will increase without any effort.

2. Abundance thrives on connection: The first point of connection is with yourself and the present moment. Making a habit of being aware of your body, your breath, and your thoughts is a start to better connecting with yourself. Connection in the present moment also takes practice. When you are fully connected in the here and now, you feel a calmness and peace. This is your being state. There is nothing to do.

The second stage of connection is in spirit. Some begin by connecting in prayer or meditation. Others find it in nature. Some feel that connection by getting their bodies moving in some way. When you can be in the space of feeling connected most all of the time, no matter where you are or what you are doing, you will notice a lot of synchronicities, and you will feel yourself in the flow.

The next stage of connection is naturally a connection with others. You will have opportunities to enter into relationships, community, and possible collaborations. In the flow of abundance, everything and everyone is connected to serve the world's higher good.

3. Abundance requires a reverent money mindset: If you are attempting to attract money in the space of unworthiness and lack, it simply will not work, and what you do attract will not last. You have to believe you are worth it, deserving, and abundant.

Also, it is important to look at how we unconsciously and consciously view money. Many of us have been raised with the limiting beliefs that "Money doesn't grow on trees," "Money is the root of all evil," "People with money are dishonest and cannot be trusted," "I can't afford it," "That is too expensive," "I don't really need money," "Money changes people," "There isn't enough to go around," and the list goes on. How are we to attract more money if our brains have been programmed to believe money is hard to come by? The answer is: reprogram your brain.

You have to believe you are worth it, deserving, and abundant.

Two people can be in the same experience, yet draw opposite conclusions. The same goes with money beliefs. If you believe and experience money as hard to come by, you will continue to relive the story of lack of money in your life because your brain grabs information that lines up with the "lack" programming. It is interesting that, no matter the economic climate, people who have an abundant mindset continue to thrive.

How do you make the massive shift to an abundant money mindset? First, be more aware of the information coming to you and choose how you want to process the information surrounding money. You can create new neuropathways to abundant belief systems with practice. It is important to consciously change how you view and speak about money. Money is simply a flow of energy. It flows in and it flows out. If you experience disempowering emotions when you have to pay bills or taxes, you can stifle the flow with your resistance. To have a reverent mindset around money, train your mind to experience joy in giving, whether it be to give in paying bills, tithing, donating to a charitable cause, or paying taxes to Uncle Sam. We get to give, and we get to receive. There is plenty of abundance to go around. As you develop a more generous attitude toward money, you will find that it flows more easily through you.

> You can create new neuropathways to abundant belief systems with practice. It is important to consciously change how you view and speak about money. Money is simply a flow of energy.

4. Giving fuels abundance: As you rise into greater purpose, you will find that a large part of your vision is to serve others in some way. The more you love and serve others, the more you will be fueled by the beautiful, intrinsic rewards that come with your karmic deposits. You will begin to see the bigger picture of your life and find that embodying a giving spirit feels good. When others are involved, it creates a steady momentum, and the universe will rise up to serve you. Notice how your ability to stay in abundant flow increases when you practice self-love, and then stand as an instrument to build others up. Serving will become the fuel for your aliveness.

The intention in giving is key here. To give expecting something in return is not the way of abundance. If you feel someone owes you when you give and serve, you are missing the point. As humans, we are moving away from extrinsic motivation tied to an archaic reward/punishment system. We are becoming more motivated intrinsically, by serving and by a vision, either ours or someone else's, with no strings attached.

> *Notice how your ability to stay in abundant flow increases when you practice self-love. Then stand as an instrument to build others up.*

5. Abundance and vision go hand in hand: To be in the flow of abundance, you have to participate in the game. The game is called, "What was I sent here to do?" When you become interested in a bigger vision for your life based on your gifts, talents, and passions, you will begin to receive signs and glimpses of what is possible. Creating your vision in a higher state, where you are deeply connected to what it feels, sounds, and looks like, and how it will change your life and the world, will naturally create abundance momentum. I will dive deeper into vision in the next and final chapter.

6. Inspired action activates the flow of abundance: Ask yourself, "What are the next inspired action steps to achieving my vision?" The key is to map out the action steps while you are deeply connected emotionally to the vision. Realize that our brains love routine and the comfort zone. To step out of your comfort zone, create achievable goals based on consistency. Start small until you create a new comfort zone; then stretch yourself more. Each time you attain a goal, your brain will emit dopamine. The satisfaction you get in taking inspired action is actually linked to a flood of dopamine, a rewarding neurotransmitter, emitted in the brain. As you accomplish inspired action steps, you will feel pulled by your vision. The key is to remain in your being state while taking the inspired action to remain in the flow of abundance. The minute you push too hard in a striving or yearning state, you will drop out of the flow.

7. Gratitude: Tony Robbins says, "Trade your expectations for appreciation and your world changes instantly." Most scientific studies associate gratitude with an overall feeling of wellbeing. By simply shifting from the mindset that you do not have enough to a mindset of gratefulness and appreciation for what you do have, you will automatically be in the flow of abundance. Researchers found the following strategies helped enhance feelings of gratitude:

- Journaling about things for which to be grateful

- Thinking about someone for whom you are grateful

- Writing a thank you note or a letter to someone for whom you are grateful

- Meditating on gratitude

- Praying with gratitude

- Reflecting at the end of each day on three things for which you are most grateful.

- Practicing saying "Thank you" in a sincere and meaningful way

Another aspect of gratitude is appreciating what you receive. This could range from someone offering a simple compliment to doing you a huge favor. How do you receive these acts of giving? For some, it may be easier to give, yet it is equally important to have a positive emotional response when you receive. Include this affirmation in your *I am* statements: I am open and ready to receive abundance. Practice receiving compliments with a genuine "Thank you." Keep in mind, too, that when people do something for you, it causes them to feel more connected to you. When someone extends a kind gesture to you or when you receive money, how do you feel? For the exchange to flow, receive with joy and express your joy so others can feel the exchange.

ABUNDANCE EXERCISES:

Self-Love/Self-Worth:

How can I practice reverence toward myself to improve my sense of self-worth?

_____

_____

_____

Connection:

What one thing can I do daily to connect to myself and the present moment?

_____

What one thing can I do daily to practice a deeper spiritual connection?

_____

What one thing can I do to connect to others?

_____

Reverent money mindset:

What affirmation can I state daily to reinforce that I am worthy, deserving, and abundant?

_____

What new language can I use around money?

_____

_____

_____

_____

_____

Giving:

How can I be more generous?

_____

_____

_____

_____

Vision:

What is my vision of living an inspired life, using my gifts to feel alive?

_____

_____

_____

_____

Inspired Action:

What are the next inspired action steps for achieving my vision?

_____

_____

_____

_____

_____

_____

Gratitude:

I am grateful for (journal about three things):

_____

_____

_____

_____

_____

_____

How can I receive money, acts of service, and compliments with joy?

_____

_____

_____

_____

If you practice these seven components—self-love; connection with yourself, the present moment, in spirit, and with others; have a reverent money mindset; give with intrinsic motivation; have a vision; take inspired action; and practice gratitude in receiving—your life will feel more effortless in the flow of true abundance.

CHAPTER 16

Building and Embodying Your Vision

If you are working on something exciting that you really care about,
you don't have to be pushed. The vision pulls you.

— STEVE JOBS

Looking back on all your learning, think about when you first started this journey. Knowing what you know now, all the rich wisdom
you have gathered, how can you now embody a more meaningful
vision and show up as a servant leader? If you haven't already, take
an inventory of your gifts and talents, and begin envisioning how
you can share them with the world. What would change in how you
lead yourself and others? Ask yourself, "What was I sent here to do?"
If you are fully unleashed into third story reverence, where you are
tapped into ultimate intuition and pure creativity, the answer will
come back loud and clear, and your vision will unfold before your
eyes. You will begin to experience synchronicities as you carry out
that vision, and it will feel more effortless because you are being
pulled by a vision bigger than you. When challenges arise, you will
be better equipped to stay in a reverent state and work through
them, allowing your intuition to guide you during the ebb and flow.

MAKE A DATE WITH TIME

Time is of the essence in embodying your vision. How you spend your time will determine greatly your success in achieving your vision. Whatever you feel pulled to bring forth, whether it be to start a business, write and publish your book, improve your health, try a new hobby—whatever it is—all it takes is making a date with time to follow through. Time will always be there. Your vision will always be there as well. You just have to open up your calendar and schedule time to bring your vision to life. The key is to make the steps you are adding into your calendar achievable and to allow room for creativity. Start small and you can always add more to it as you gain confidence in the flow. Our brains emit dopamine when we achieve our goals. Your brain will love the process, and your future self will thank you for taking the first, small steps.

Your brain will love the process, and your future self will thank you for taking the first, small steps.

A VISION BLUEPRINT

Step 1: Define your "why." Before we get into building your vision and mapping out the strategy to get there, it is important to ask yourself, "Why is this so important to me? Who will my vision effect? How will my vision change my life, my loved ones, and the world?" When you have a clear picture of why it is crucial for you to rise into this new vision, it will become easier to fulfill. Otherwise, your brain will keep you stuck in your comfort zones and the debilitating thought processes that make you question whether you are good enough, worthy enough, or smart enough to fulfill your vision. Your "why" will pull you because it takes the focus off of you. It takes you from the disempowering stages of first story into the unleashing, giving you the confidence to carry it through, and into the compassionate, altruistic parts of yourself that truly want to make a difference. Reminding yourself of your "why" will help you snap out of feeling unmotivated to fulfill the steps to get there.

Reminding yourself of your "why" will help you snap out of feeling unmotivated to fulfill the steps to get there.

YOUR "WHY" EXERCISE:

What is my "why"? Why is this important to me? Who will my vision affect, and how will it change my life and others' lives?

_____

_____

_____

_____

_____

_____

_____

Step 2: Visualization. After connecting to your true "why," you will be ready to build your vision. Vision-building can be either an exciting or overwhelming process, depending on how you do it. The problem is that most people are creating the steps for this new vision using the logical planning parts of their brains, rather than their creative, visual, intuitive parts. Before you plan a strategy, you must create a vision of your goal so when you schedule the step for achieving it, you are infusing creative energy into that commitment. You want to taste, hear, see, smell, and feel the end goal. I use visualization with my clients, and when we are done, they feel as if they have actually stood in the moment when they reached their end goal. They feel it to the core. This visualization technique is common in Navy Seal training and is used by Olympic athletes. To accomplish your vision, you must first visualize it to your core, as if it has already happened. Visualizing sets the framework for time management and accountability to keep you on schedule. Using visualization, your brain creates a memory of achieving your goal as if it has already happened, so when you take steps toward your goals, each step is already infused in your unconscious along with the end result.

When I work with clients, their visions are so profound that they are able to return to the feeling that encompasses that vision anytime, and it serves as a pulling force into their mission and acts as an accountability system for their action steps. When you are guided to align your heart with your brain, your mission becomes cemented into your psyche.

Using visualization, your brain creates a memory of achieving your goal as if it has already happened, so when you take steps toward your goals, each step is already infused in your unconscious along with the end result.

VISION EXERCISE:

What does your vision look like, feel like, taste like, smell like, and sound like?

_____

_____

_____

_____

_____

_____

_____

_____

Step 3: Discover the resistance. While you are creating a vision, you can discover blocks or resistance. Since you are in your higher self, in a fully relaxed state, it is easier to recognize the unconscious beliefs that are not aligned in truth and release them.

I was working with a client who asked, "Well, who am I to get up on stage and tell my story? What do I have to give?" When I asked, "Is this belief rooted in truth?" the reply was, of course, "No." Immediately, the client laughed a joyful laugh. I was also deep into the vision, and we both wholeheartedly laughed and agreed that that belief sounded silly. We discovered an unconscious belief the ego had conjured up as a protection mechanism. We could recognize it right away as not belonging to his true, authentic self. We discovered why his conscious and unconscious mind chose to align with that story. Then we wrapped it all in gratitude, released it, and let it go.

RESISTANCE EXERCISE:

What blocks or resistance do I have to my vision? What is the root of it? Am I ready to let this go? When am I ready to let this go?

_____

_____

_____

_____

_____

_____

_____

Use the compassion and gratitude exercise in Chapter 4 to release this resistance.

Step 4: Write a letter. When you are in your creative, intuitive state, write a letter to yourself from the future to your present self, congratulating yourself on achieving the goal and praising yourself on how you stayed committed to getting there. This exercise is powerful when working with authors. When they write their vision letter from the future, where their book is in hand and they are physically seeing, hearing, and feeling the impact of their message, they are creating a memory in their minds of a future event. Since your brain does not know the difference between what you imagine and reality, when it comes time to open your calendar to honor the process of that future vision, it becomes easier. You become pulled by the impact, pulled by your legacy, pulled by each and every life that you will transform. The reason the vision letter works is because you are writing out the next chapter of your life. You are the author of the legacy you deserve to leave. No matter if you are an entrepreneur, CEO, spouse, parent, author, healer, creative thought leader, or speaker, you are igniting your story, which will, in turn, ignite others. The key is to read your letter out loud every day to keep yourself inspired and to continue to imprint this vision into your unconscious mind so you are better aligned with attracting it.

MY VISION LETTER:

Write a letter from your future self, congratulating yourself on stretching outside of your comfort zone, sticking to it, and achieving your vision. Include how all aspects of your life are positively impacted.

_____

_____

_____

_____

_____

_____

_____

_____

_____

_____

_____

_____

_____

_____

Step 5: Plan. Now it is time to plan out your journey. Stay in the inspired vision while you map out the structure and goals. Reverse-engineer your vision. Now that you have stepped into your vision and can fully feel the effects of it, immediately break down the vision to achievable goals over the timeframe you expect to accomplish it. If part of your vision is to improve your relationship, look at your calendar and ask yourself, "How have I been prioritizing my time, and what can I do to make my relationship a priority on a consistent basis?" If it is to increase your business, ask yourself, "How many hours per week am I working, and how can I become more productive?"

I find in my coaching that people can get very ambitious with what they feel they can accomplish. They map out the steps and put an aggressive timeline on it. They go 100 miles per hour when previously they were only going five miles per hour. Work with your coach and put your vision on a timeline. Figure out how many hours in the week you can actually commit to it. Then map out the steps and the timeline of when you can realistically achieve it, given all your other responsibilities. Set small, bite-size goals, and show up consistently to follow through. Adjust as necessary if you get off track, and most importantly, allow room for the creative process to unfold.

MY PLAN:

What will it take to break this down into achievable, month-by-month, week-by-week steps?

_____

_____

_____

_____

_____

_____

_____

Step 6: Declare Your Goal. By declaring your goal, you are crystalizing it into reality. You are also stepping into your empowerment. Whether it be publishing your book, producing a film, expanding your business, a health and wellness goal, giving up alcohol or sugar, or attracting love, when you declare your goal to the world, you create the momentum for it to come to fruition. You are overcoming fear by reciting out loud the plan you want to achieve. That, in itself, is empowering. I believe it is an absolute myth that if you have a big dream, you are more likely to achieve it if you keep it to yourself. By speaking it into existence, the world knows you are ready for it. You will begin to attract the mentors and resources to help make your vision happen. With the public declaration, you become more invested and hold yourself accountable. And others will help hold you accountable as well.

MY DECLARATION:

How will you declare your vision? On what platforms will you declare it? Write out your declaration, including the month or season and year you plan to achieve your vision.

_____

_____

_____

_____

_____

_____

_____

Step 7: Just do it. The best way to overcome hesitation or fear is just to start. You will gain confidence in the doing. Take out a calendar and schedule in the steps to achieve your vision. Discover what is working for you in your new routine, and tweak it as you go along. Map out your weekly commitments and schedule. Once you simply start, you will begin to feel more confident in the process. You may find, as you begin executing your plan, that there are temporary setbacks. When life slows you down, it is usually a teachable moment that is serving you in ways you may not understand. Allow those moments. Then, when you feel called to it again, reengage the flow of creation to consistently bring your vision to fruition.

> ### *The best way to overcome hesitation or fear is just to start. You will gain confidence in the doing.*

If you continue to find resistance happening or feel stuck in achieving these steps toward your goals, do some introspective work to find out where the block is coming from. Sometimes we just require accountability, collaborative strategizing, and borrowing the belief from a coach and/or a community. No matter what it is, it typically comes down to our ego or inner bully attempting to keep us small.

TAMING THE EGO

People battle themselves constantly, attempting to do away with the ego. The ego is valuable. It protects us from harm. It keeps us safe and comfortable. It can become a motivator for us if we listen. The problem arises when the ego takes over. The saying goes: "Ego is an acronym for *edging God out*." Typically, the ego will create stories in our heads that are not true. As we become more conscious, we can more easily decipher what is actually true, and we can prove the ego wrong. For example, the ego may tell us we are not good enough to lead a company or speak our message from a stage. It will come up with every excuse for why it is safest not to stretch ourselves. One of the most effective ways to tame the ego is by staying in integrity with ourselves. If we can challenge the ego by staying in integrity with the inner knowing that we can, in fact, launch that business, lead that team effectively, influence people through film, write a book, or speak on stage, then we will find ourselves acting confidently upon our inspiration rather than allowing the ego to prove itself right.

Rising into greater purpose will challenge the ego. As we prove to ourselves that we can do it, the ego does not have as much ammunition against us. However, it will find new ammunition when things do not go as planned or we struggle to stay in integrity with our vision. This is why it is so important to constantly be reminding ourselves of our "why" and using visualization daily to stay connected to the big vision. The most imperative thing to note is that this voice inside your head—which compares you to others, causes you to get offended easily, tells you to give up when things get difficult, tells you people are out to get you, and tells you that you are not good enough—is not you. This is your inner bully. Ask yourself: "Who is listening to or observing the ego's voice?" The answer is you, your higher, conscious self. When you realize you are not the voice of the ego, it becomes easier to shift toward simply observing the ego. One way to recognize you are not the voice is simply to sit outside and focus on nature. When thoughts enter your mind, simply observe them. Take inventory of every dream and aspiration. Ask yourself: "What is holding me back from taking steps toward this dream?" What comes up is the ego's favorite disguise…the comfort zone.

Rising into greater purpose will challenge the ego. As we prove to ourselves that we can do it, the ego does not have as much ammunition against us.

One common theme regarding ego that I see in my coaching is people's fear that if they become successful and abundant, their ego will inflate. The best way to deflate this notion is to find the greater purpose behind all you are doing and recognize that the stronger you stand in your vision, with a voice to create change, the more people you will affect. Whom would it serve for you to continue to play small? The answer is the ego. You have to ask your ego to stand aside so your authentic voice can shine through. If you allow the ego to continue to pilot the ship, you are missing out on being a key component for people's transformations. Whether you are writing a book, creating a transformational film, improving how you lead at work, or coaching your kid's basketball team, whenever you step outside of your comfort zone, you are standing in a servant role. As long as you are serving and using your abundance for good, you can keep the ego in check.

Realize all that transpires as you level up into a bigger vision for your life is part of the process, molding you into your higher self.

Here is where surrender comes in. Listen to the still, quiet voice that tells you it is time to make a shift, to practice self-love, to carve out more time with your family, to wake up earlier to write that book, to take a break, to change your health lifestyle, to walk through this door of opportunity, etc. Honor the process. Realize that all that transpires as you level up into a bigger vision for your life is part of the process, molding you into your higher self. I found that as I set out to do something to stretch myself, there was always something more to learn and a divine timing in place. Know that you may start out strategizing your plan one way, only to find it takes a turn into something else. You deserve all the learning that comes with each part of your journey. You will intuitively know when it is time to take the next steps. Everything will unveil itself to you when you are ready. This is a part of the surrendering. The most important part is to listen. As you are in the flow of creation, you will intuitively know when to take steps and when to pause. Step by step, you will begin to step out of your comfort zone and develop a new comfort zone as you grow the confidence to honor the vision that pulls you.

CELEBRATION IS KEY

In order to elevate and reinforce our joyful experiences, it is imperative that we celebrate more. We are conditioned in this society to avoid shining the spotlight on ourselves, to downplay our gifts and talents, and to lower ourselves so we blend in with everyone else. This keeps us from rising. What message are we sending? As we stretch ourselves into a more reverent, purposeful life, we must be willing to celebrate every step along the way. Even if we fail, we can celebrate our hard work, effort, and the lessons we learned. What if we shifted our perception and could see everything in life as a cause for celebration?

What if we shifted our perception and could see everything in life as a cause for celebration?

Make celebration lists for various aspects of your life: your relationships, your childhood, past failures, your health, finances, spiritual life, leadership roles, and your legacy.

How are you authentically celebrating all of yourself and the person you are? Stop and breathe into that. As you rise further into your vision to share your gifts and talents to the world, celebrate yourself and your entire story as whole and complete.

Journal below what you can celebrate about your past experiences:

_____

_____

_____

_____

_____

_____

_____

_____

Journal below what you can celebrate about yourself and your life right now:

_____

_____

_____

_____

_____

_____

_____

_____

Most importantly, celebrate who are rising up to be. You are ready. You are strong. Rise. The world deserves you!

CONCLUSION

It is my hope that I have fulfilled my intention for this book to provide the breakthroughs and direction you have been searching for to exercise stronger self-leadership and positively impact the way you lead others and ignite your story. It is my wish that you can now lead your life fully unleashed, with a positive mindset, better connected with your intuition, your creative expression, and a more powerful vision for your life.

I believe that with intentional daily practice, *Unleash Your Rising* can gift you with the ability to lead with reverent intention in all aspects of your life. You are now equipped with the tools to let go of limiting beliefs and emotions that no longer serve you. When you are challenged, you can apply the Acknowledge, Release, and Intend (ARI) steps to command the situation and turn it around. You can now rise above your story, and live out the next chapter of your story in the flow of abundance.

My life passion is to ignite the pure creativity and authentic voice within you that has been begging to be heard and expressed. Through what you learn on your journey, you can become resilient and stronger, standing in your story as a way to connect more authentically in your leadership and relationships. It is my personal mission to empower you to turn every feeling of unworthiness and lack into a powerful story that moves others.

I invite you, no matter the stage you are in, to consistently review the responses and perceptions you are taking on in your daily life. Align them with peace, gratitude, and celebration. Allow the learning to unveil itself during the challenging times, rather than covering it up with distractions. If something comes up from the past, revisit it only to fully release it, and take that opportunity to climb higher in *Your Story of Intention* from disempowerment to reverence.

Listen to the answers that come back when you ask, "Am I in integrity with my higher good, and am I fulfilling my mission?" May the still inner knowing be activated within you so you become pulled by it, grow stronger in your spiritual connection, become more deeply connected in your leadership capabilities, and serve the transformation of humanity.

Be willing to do whatever it takes to activate your voice and use it to inspire others and ignite purpose in your life. You are meant to make your mark and elevate the world. You are built for greatness. You just have to unleash into it. Become fueled by what inspires you each morning and as you go about your day, every day. The metamorphosis is the hardest part, but all along, you are being directed toward something more aligned with your true essence.

Truly listen to the nudges calling you to stand in courage in writing your book, making your movie, launching your business, transforming how you lead, and becoming a more conscious and connected human being. Live intentionally. Be expectant of what is in store.

I believe that as you embrace being unleashed, you will become a vessel for a message that encourages interconnection and change. The stories of your life are infused with purpose. You may not see the full picture yet of who you are, how you will rise into your message, or where your path is leading because you are a painting on the canvas in the making. Living in the flow of creative inspiration will continually unveil the core of who you are and why you are here. As you shift into gratitude and a reverence for your entire journey, the purposeful leader within you will become unleashed. That leader will begin to rise within you like the sun that rises upon the earth to illuminate its beauty and all its gifts.

RISING IN PURPOSE AND COMMUNITY

I alone cannot change the world, but I can cast a stone
across the waters to create many ripples.

- MOTHER TERESA

It gives me the greatest joy to see this message create a ripple effect. You can experience the joy of witnessing the transformation of your friends, family, and colleagues by sharing and recommending *Unleash Your Rising*. I encourage you to build community around this movement through an *Unleash Your Rising* book club or discussion group. Bulk copies of *Unleash Your Rising* can be purchased by visiting www. UnleashYourRising.com/book. Also visit www.UnleashYourRising.com/ resources to receive your free *Unleash Your Rising* resources, including the color *Your Story of Intention* chart, guided visualizations, writing and publishing tips, and to join my private community. Let's rise together!

UNLEASH POSITIVE CHANGE IN YOUR ORGANIZATION:

Unleash Your Rising: Lead with Intention and Ignite Your Story

KEYNOTE, WORKSHOP, EVENT, OR TRAINING

Your employees, managers, followers, members, or students can experience inspired and profound change from Christine Gail's *Unleash Your Rising* message in a live group workshop, training, event, or keynote.

Your team will not only feel more motivated in their work, but they will also be empowered with tools to improve their mindsets, creative bandwidth, personal and work relationships, and ability to tap into a deeper vision that pulls them.

The *Unleash Your Rising* message will help them achieve greater success, become more resilient and productive, and ignite the leader within themselves. Attendees report feeling a renewed passion for their lives and an enhanced ability to connect with others and achieve extraordinary results.

Christine Gail delivers a customized message with program materials catered toward your organization's vision. Follow-up personal or remote training can also be designed. *The Unleash Your Rising* Keynote, Workshop, Event, or Training is ideal for:

- Managers and executives
- Independent sales professionals
- Corporate groups and new hires
- Work-at-home employees and telecommuters
- Students, educators, and school administrators
- Nonprofit managers and employees
- Women's retreats
- Employees facing layoffs
- Entrepreneurs, filmmakers, and authors
- Small business owners
- Leadership conferences

To learn more, go to ChristineGail.com or
email christine@unleashyourrising.com

EVERYONE HAS A BOOK IN THEM

Best-Selling Author Book Publishing Program by Christine Gail

When you get your book out into the world, you are leaving a legacy that can impact generations to come. Whether you want to utilize your book as a lead-generating tool to speak your message from stage, as a way to build credibility and momentum in your business, or to simply get your story out to the world to transform lives, you must have a strategy in place in order to fulfill your vision.

Christine Gail inspires authors to rise into a more significant vision for their book and provides a simple step-by-step program to break the book process down from writing, to editing, to publishing, to best seller, and to next steps into achievable segments.

Her program offers guidance on the following:

- Structuring and writing your book
- Creating a winning title formula
- Strategizing writing accountability and a book launch plan
- Building your following
- Choosing traditional or self-publishing
- Applying the best-seller formula
- Selling your book in bulk
- Gaining worldwide distribution in bookstores and libraries
- Adapting your book to film
- Using your book as a lead-generating tool for coaching and consulting
- Increasing your income through paid speaking engagements

To learn more about this program visit:
www.UnleashYourRising.com/publishing.

ACKNOWLEDGMENTS

This book has been greatly enriched by the influences of The HeartMath Institute, Dr. Wayne Dyer, Dr. David Hawkins, Eckhart Tolle, Gary Zukav, Oprah Winfrey, Brené Brown, Jack Canfield, John Assaraf's Brain-A-Thon, and various other teachers cited within these pages. I express immense appreciation to Barnet Bain for his impact on my work and for helping me realize my creative potential. I acknowledge everyone involved in the process of bringing this book to life: my brilliant editors Tyler Tichelaar and Larry Alexander and my creative designers Shiloh Schroeder, Rachel Langaker, and Sherdellah Anunciado. I am filled with gratitude for Les Brown giving me a profound moment of realization that I can be a bolder speaker. I am deeply grateful for the support, friendship, and mentorship provided by my publishing coach Patrick Snow, my transformational coach Jenn Beninger, and accountability business coach Megan Unsworth.

Thank you to my heavenly Creator, my dear friends, my entire family, and my faith and mastermind communities for their love, support, and belief in my work. I extend a special thank you to Stephanie Martin for her generosity in allowing me to use her pool house as a writing sanctuary. I would like to convey sincere gratitude and love to my husband Dr. Chris Hengesteg, for his patience and support while I poured myself into this book and for his nurturing influence on my body and soul.

REFERENCES

Ch. 1: Your Story Matters

- *The Third Story: Awakening the Love that Transforms* by Barnet Bain
- *Daring Greatly: How the Courage to Be Vulnerable Transforms the Way We Live, Love, Parent, and Lead* by Brene' Brown
- *The Seven Basic Plots: Why We Tell Stories* by Christopher Booker
- *Leadersight: Seeing the Invisible to Create the Impossible* by Pastor Jurgen Matthesius

Ch. 3: Your Story of Intention, Part 2: Unleashing

- Integrity: http://ssrn.com/abstract=1511274
- *Power vs. Force: The Hidden Determinants of Human Behavior* by Dr. David Hawkins
- *Success Is for You: Using Heart-Centered Power Principles for Lasting Abundance and Fulfillment* by Dr. David Hawkins
- *A New Earth* and *The Power of Now* by Eckhart Tolle

Ch. 4: Your Story of Intention, Part 3: Reverence

- Ho'oponopono prayer: https://healingearth.info/hooponopono/
- *The Shift*, documentary by Dr. Wayne Dyer

Ch. 5: Listening to the Still, Quiet Voice

- *The Power of Intention* by Dr. Wayne Dyer

Ch. 7: Your Superpower of Intention and Language

- NLP for limiting beliefs:
    - http://www.thelawofattraction.com/subconscious-influence/
    - http://nlppractitioner.uk.com/nlp-practitioner-you-see-what-you-believe/
- *The Hidden Messages in Water* by Dr. Masuru Emoto
- HeartMath Institute: https://www.heartmath.org
- "Modulation of DNA Conformation by Heart-Focused Intention" http://laszlo.ind.br/admin/artigos/arquivos/ModulacaodoDNApelaenergiadasmaos.pdf

Ch. 8: Letting Go

- *The Psychology of Achievement* by Brian Tracy
- *The Tapping Solution for Manifesting Your Greatest Self* by Nick Ortner
- Forgiveness: https://www.mayoclinic.org/healthy-lifestyle/adult-health/in-depth/forgiveness/art-20047692
- *When I Was Young, I Said I Would Be Happy*, documentary produced by Barnet Bain, Lori Leyden, and Nicolas M. Ortner

Ch. 9: The Power of Affirmations

- https://productivitytheory.com/science-self-affirmations/
- *The Best of Les Brown Audio Collection: Inspiration from the World's Leading Motivational Speaker* by Les Brown

Ch. 10: Understanding the Brain to Facilitate Life Change

- *The Power of the Heart* documentary, written and directed by Drew Heriot. Produced by Alain De Levita.
- Meditation:
    - https://www.ncbi.nlm.nih.gov/pmc/articles/PMC526201/

- · https://www.newscientist.com/article/2149489-different-meditation-types-train-distinct-parts-of-your-brain/
- · https://www.ncbi.nlm.nih.gov/pmc/articles/PMC3004979
- Gamma brain waves:
  - · https://blog.mindvalley.com/gamma-brain-waves/
  - · http://brainwavewizard.com/entrainment/the-benefits-of-gamma-brainwaves/
  - · https://www.ibcsr.org/index.php/institute-research-portals/spirituality-and-health-causation-project/557-gamma-waves-may-be-meditation-s-tool-for-changing-the-brain
- Compassion and Loving Kindness Meditation:
  - · https://centerhealthyminds.org/news/training-your-compassion-muscle-may-boost-brains-resilience-in-the-face-of-suffering
  - · https://www.huffpost.com/entry/how-you-can-train-your-mi_n_3688660
  - · https://emmaseppala.com/18-science-based-reasons-try-loving-kindness-meditation-today/

Ch. 11: Living a Healthy Life

- Alkaline: https://liveenergized.com/wp-content/uploads/2015/06/alkaline-food-chart-4.0.pdf
- Choline: https://www.livestrong.com/article/212268-what-is-choline-bitartrate/
- Omega-3s:
  - · https://www.ncbi.nlm.nih.gov/pmc/articles/PMC4404917/
  - · https://www.webmd.com/diet/supplement-guide-omega-3-fatty-acids#1

- Turmeric:
    - https://www.ncbi.nlm.nih.gov/books/NBK92752/
    - https://www.organicfacts.net/health-benefits/herbs-and-spices/turmeric.html
    - https://www.mindbodygreen.com/0-6873/25-Reasons-Why-Turmeric-Can-Heal-You.html
- Ashwaganda: https://www.healthline.com/nutrition/12-proven-ashwagandha-benefits#section3
- Coffee Berry:
    - https://ghr.nlm.nih.gov/gene/BDNF
    - http://www.futureceuticals.com/products/neurofactor
    - http://www.coffeeberry.com/initial-research-0
- Lions mane: https://www.ncbi.nlm.nih.gov/pubmed/26244378
- Magnesium: https://www.naturalstacks.com/blogs/news/magnesium
- CoQ-10: https://www.ncbi.nlm.nih.gov/pmc/articles/PMC21173/
- B vitamins:
    - https://articles.mercola.com/sites/articles/archive/2016/03/17/vitamin-b-brain-health.aspx
    - https://www.ncbi.nlm.nih.gov/pmc/articles/PMC4772032/
- Brain supplements: https://www.consciouslifestylemag.com/brain-health-key-supplements-habits/
- Sugar:
    - https://www.ncbi.nlm.nih.gov/pubmed/23719144
    - https://www.livestrong.com/article/496016-sugar-cravings-are-a-sign-of-which-mineral-deficiency/

- http://www.organicauthority.com/ spices-that-naturally-stop-sugar-cravings/
- https://www.huffingtonpost.com/gabrielle-bernstein/ spiritual-tips-for-quitti_b_4661071.html

- BDNF: https://www.ncbi.nlm.nih.gov/pubmed/17151862
- Sleep:
  - https://blog.bufferapp.com/how-naps-affect-your-brain-and-why-you-should-have-one-every-day
  - https://www.ncbi.nlm.nih.gov/pubmed/21075238
- *Biology of Belief* by Bruce Lipton

Ch. 12: A Self-Leadership Roadmap

- Integrity: http://ssrn.com/abstract=1511274
- *The Success Principles: How to Get From Where You Are to Where You Want to Be* by Jack Canfield

Ch. 13: Leading with Intention

- Meditation and Mindfulness:
  - http://advances.sciencemag.org/content/3/10/e1700489
  - https://www.newscientist.com/article/2149489-different-meditation-types-train-distinct-parts-of-your-brain/
  - https://hbr.org/2015/12/how-meditation-benefits-ceos.
  - Reb, J et al. "Mindfulness at work: Antecedents and consequences of employee awareness and absent mindedness." *Mindfulness.* 2013; 6 (1): 111-122.
  - Reb, J et al. "Leading mindfully: two studies on the influence of supervisor trait mindfulness on employee wellbeing and performance." *Mindfulness.* 2012; 5 (1): 36-45.
  - http://themindfulnessinitiative.org.uk/images/reports/ MI_Building-the-Case_v1.1_Oct16.pdf

- Freedom in work:
  - https://hbr.org/2014/01/employees-perform-better-when-they-can-control-their-space
  - *Did I Ever Tell You How Lucky You Are?* by Dr. Seuss
- Celebration: http://theutopianlife.com/2014/10/14/hacking-into-your-happy-chemicals-dopamine-serotonin-endorphins-oxytocin/
- Fun at work: http://www.onrec.com/news/statistics-and-trends/new-study-reveals-fun-at-work-can-boost-productivity-and-reduce-sick-days
- Employee satisfaction and retention: https://www.pay-scale.com/content/whitepaper/wp_EmployeeExperience.pdf?utm_source=Marketo&utm_medium=email&utm_campaign=
- Employee appreciation: https://www.businessnewsdaily.com/8152-employee-appreciation-tips.html
- Millennials at work:
  - https://www.forbes.com/sites/sarahland-rum/2017/09/15/how-learning-leads-to-happiness-for-millennials/2/#7eb89bfa1ede
  - https://news.gallup.com/opinion/gallup/221024/why-best-millennials-leave-keep.aspx
- *Dare to Lead: Brave Work. Tough Conversations. Whole Hearts.* by Brene' Brown

Ch. 14: Tapping into Pure Creativity

- *The Book of Doing and Being: Rediscovering Creativity in Life, Love, and Work* by Barnet Bain
- Exercise: http://www.pnas.org/content/108/7/3017.full

Ch. 15: Being in the Flow of Abundance

- Goals and dopamine: https://www.psychologyto-day.com/us/blog/the-truisms-wellness/201610/the-science-accomplishing-your-goals

- Gratitude: https://www.ncbi.nlm.nih.gov/pmc/articles/PMC3010965/

Ch. 16: Building and Embodying Your Vision

- Visualization: https://theweek.com/articles/617474/4-techniques-navy-seals-olympians-use-mental-toughness
- *The Little Book of Talent: 52 Tips for Improving Your Skills* by Via Coyle
- Goal-setting: https://www.scienceofpeople.com/goal-setting/
- *Innercise: The New Science to Unlock Your Brain's Hidden Power* by John Assaraf
- Celebration: https://brainleadersandlearners.com/2011/10/30/a-brain-on-celebration

ABOUT THE AUTHOR

CHRISTINE GAIL is an author, keynote speaker, leadership strategist, and story breakthrough book publishing coach with a mission to ignite a deeper purpose in others. She offers profound insights into the power of story and has proven that everyone can become a more impactful leader of their own life and in their work by rising into a more whole and complete perception of their story. Her *Unleash Your Rising* message includes using the authentic power of intention while understanding the inner workings of the successful mind, emotional intelligence, and the psychology of vision-building. Christine combines more than two decades of business development experience, an English degree from Rutgers University, and various mindset and breakthrough techniques to advise and mentor authors, creative thought leaders, top executives, and entrepreneurs. Christine enjoys inspiring people to unleash their leadership potential and ignite their creative gifts to make a constructive impact on the world. She lives in San Diego with her husband and their two daughters.

FOR MORE INFORMATION ABOUT CHRISTINE GAIL:
ChristineGail.com
UnleashYourRising.com

FOLLOW CHRISTINE ON SOCIAL MEDIA:
facebook.com/unleashyourrising
YouTube: Christine Gail
Instagram: @christine_gail7
#unleashyourrising

SPEAKING, COACHING, and MEDIA INQUIRIES:
ChristineGail.com
christine@unleashyourrising.com